Blackpool to Fleetwood

Part 1: The Tramroad Builders

IN the year 1895, the seaside wateringplace of Blackpool was on the brink of a remarkable period of expansion, which in less than a decade was to double the size of the town and establish it beyond dispute as the foremost popular holiday resort in Britain. Not only was the holiday trade booming, but improved railway services had brought the Fylde coast within commuting distance of the cotton towns of Lancashire, and the area was ripe for a massive increase in residential development.

The first railway in the Fylde, the Preston & Wyre Railway, was opened on July 15th 1840 and ran direct to the new port of Fleetwood. Passengers for the small sea-bathing resort of Blackpool had to alight at Poulton-le-Fylde and continue by road, until a four-mile branch line was opened from Poulton into Blackpool on April 29 1846. The second railway in Blackpool entered from the south, and was opened on April 4 1863; its operators, the Blackpool & Lytham Railway, sought powers in 1864 to continue it northwards along the coast to Fleetwood, but these were rejected, and the seven-mile coastal stretch between the Gynn Inn at North Shore, Blackpool, and the outskirts of Fleetwood remained desolate, remote and completely undeveloped. Blackpool itself ended abruptly at the Gynn Inn, where the coastline was interrupted by a large defile.

The idea of developing the northern cliffs was by no means new, for it had been canvassed during the last property boom in Blackpool in the mid-1870s. In 1877 a scheme was announced by a Manchester syndicate for an 18-mile steam tramway along the coast from Lytham to Fleetwood. It was surveyed and planned by Benjamin Corless Sykes, a local man who had made his name in Blackpool in the 1860s when his firm, Garlick, Park & Sykes of Preston had built the great new Promenade from Talbot Square to South Shore. By 1895 Sykes was a wealthy man, and amongst his many interests were several important land holdings between Blackpool and Fleetwood.

Sykes made enough money to hand over much of the day-to-day running of his company (now renamed Garlick & Sykes) to his chief lieutenant, Tom G. Lumb. Lumb was a Yorkshireman who, like Sykes, combined professional ability as an engineer, surveyor and architect, with a flair for development and a great enthusiasm for town planning. And Lumb had a vision. He saw the coast between Blackpool and Fleetwood dotted with well-planned 'garden estates' carefully planned and linked together to Blackpool and Fleetwood by an equally well-planned highway running alongside a modern high-speed electric tramway. The tramway, Lumb believed, was the key to a successful suburban development, and in this belief he was years ahead of his time, at least in Britain. In the USA electric tramways and real-estate development went hand-in-hand, and Lumb believed firmly in the American approach, combined with strict control of each estate. 'The best town planner', he once said, 'is a light railway or tramway'.

The two engineers had little difficulty in deciding the route which the line would

---

Opposite:
The Blackpool and Fleetwood Tramroad before the tracks were joined in 1920 with those of Blackpool Corporation. Present-day references on the map refer to 1958, when this map was drawn. The later evolution of the Dickson Road/Talbot Road junction layout is illustrated on page 47.
(J. C. Gillham)

On the cover:
Blackpool Pantograph car 170, the last of the class to remain in passenger service, at the Gynn during an enthusiasts' tour in the summer of 1961. (B. R. Turner)

take. They seem to have followed the same route which Sykes had surveyed in 1877, along the coast to Rossall and then straight across the fields to Fleetwood. For most of its route, the line would be on land in which Sykes and Lumb already had an interest, for they had established an 'empire' which reached into most corners of the Fylde coast. All they had to do was obtain entry into Blackpool and raise the money.

The land around Fleetwood, as far south as Rossall, was owned by the Fleetwood Estate Company, of which Lumb soon became managing director. At Rossall the route of the tramway entered the Thornton Estate, whose agent at that time was Benjamin Sykes, and just to the south of Cleveleys it entered the 25-acre grounds of Eryngo Lodge, which Sykes had bought and planned to extend into a 60-bedroom hydropathic hotel. Through Anchorsholme and Little Bispham several small landowners were involved, including the Norbreck Hall Hotel, and then the line entered the Norbreck Estate which reached along the cliffs past Bispham. Benjamin Sykes owned the Norbreck Estate, formed a company in 1896 to develop the land, and arranged for the tramway to pay £1000 for its share of the land. Immediately next to the Norbreck Estate lay the Gynn Estate which stretched down to the Blackpool boundary, and Tom Lumb acted as advisor to the syndicate which controlled the Gynn Estate . All in all, it was a very neatly tied-up package.

Fleetwood was enthusiastic about the line, because it would provide competition for the monopolistic railway company, and the only real hurdle which the promoters had to overcome was the attitude of Blackpool Council, who preferred to keep complete control of the town's public transport after their take-over of the Blackpool Electric Tramway Company in 1892. Somehow, Blackpool had to be persuaded to build a line from the town centre to meet the Fleetwood line at the boundary.

Fortunately, Sykes and Lumb had a trump card, or rather the Gynn Estate Company had. The Corporation needed a ready source of filling material for their scheme to build a new sea-wall and artificial promenades reclaimed from the sea along Claremont Park. The Gynn Estate, whose land lay at the end of the new Promenade, contained ample spare material for the Corporation works. An agreement was reached whereby the Corporation took over all the Estate's land within the borough boundary and would take from it the filling material, con-

Norbreck Hydro and Norbreck Hall viewed across the Fleetwood Tramroad about 1906, with car 16 bound for Blackpool visible on the extreme left. Norbreck Hall, one of the few buildings on the coast that pre-dated the Tramroad, had become a private hotel by 1898. The adjacent "hydropathic establishment" was built in 1899, and a new road was built from Bispham to this point by the estate company. There was no coast road beyond Norbreck until 1932.

(Commercial postcard courtesy J. H. Price

veniently eliminating the high cliffs just north of the Gynn, and agreed in return to build a tramway from Talbot Road Station to the beginning of the Gynn Estate and a new road up the regraded hill from the Gynn to the boundary. This suited the tramway promoters, for it gave them an assured entry into Blackpool.

In May 1896 the Corporation agreed to grant a 21-year lease of this line to the Fleetwood syndicate, and the Blackpool and Fleetwood Tramroad Act 1896 was then passed unopposed. The use of the term "tramroad" may have been due to the fact that this Act preceded by a few weeks the passing of the Light Railways Act 1896 which gave legal significance to the term "light railway"; a later ruling by the House of Lords defined a tramroad as *"a tramway laid elsewhere than along a street or road"*. The private right-of-way section of the Fleetwood route is still known as "the tramroad".

The prospectus of the Blackpool & Fleetwood Tramroad Company was published in early June 1897. The share capital was to be £120 000, with authorised borrowing powers of £40 000, and the prospectus stated that contracts for the permanent way and buildings had been let to Dick, Kerr & Co Ltd of Kilmarnock, and for the electrical equipment to Mather & Platt Ltd of Salford Iron Works, Manchester. The tramroad portion of the line would be held by the company in perpetuity, and the gauge would be 4ft 8½in. Construction was placed in the hands of the General Tramroad Maintenance & Construction Company, established by Sykes in 1896, and the financial arrangements were carried out by Benjamin Sykes' co-promoter, T. S. Turnbull, a Manchester solicitor who had a house at St. Annes. Turnbull obviously had enormous business influence, for not only did he raise the capital with no trouble at all, but he assembled a team of directors who between them already controlled an impressive proportion of the British tramway industry.

A start was made on the construction of the tramroad at the Fleetwood end on July 19 1897, and about 400 navvies were engaged on the works. In August the company commenced building car sheds at Fleetwood in a field on the Copse and, on September 8, Fleetwood Council approved the design for the central standards intended to support the overhead in Fleetwood streets. Whereas Blackpool was to construct and maintain the route in its area and lease it to the company, Fleetwood allowed the company to build its own street tramway, the Council receiving no rental but reserving the right to purchase the Fleetwood portion after 30 years.

Meanwhile, phenomenal progress had been made on the construction of the company's line. At that time, there were no roads alongside the route of the "tramroad" section. All constructional materials had to be carried forward on the rails as the formation was prepared, the contractors using small steam locomotives. Between the Gynn and Anchorsholme there were cuttings of up to 16 feet deep involving 123 000 cubic yards of excavation, much of it through tough boulder clay necessitating blasting. There were ten level crossings, seven of which were on public roads and all provided with cattle guards. An unclimbable iron fence protected the tramroad throughout its length. By February 18 1898, the double-track tramroad between Blackpool boundary and Ash Street, Fleetwood, was laid. Street track in Fleetwood was one-third finished and Bispham generating station was almost completed despite severe damage caused by a gale. At the end of February, a trial run over the 6 miles 480 yards of tramroad by a contractor's locomotive was accomplished in 17 minutes.

The Corporation's contractor, Edward Nicholls, who had just built the conduit line in Station Road, South Shore, began work on the Blackpool section in October 1897, after an urgent reminder from Garlick & Sykes. From the boundary just south of the Cabin, this portion was paved with wood blocks and laid in grooved rail. At the Gynn the line left its unfenced roadside reservation and veered round the old Gynn Inn before climbing up what was then Warbreck Road (renamed Dickson Road in 1927) and entering the built-up part of Blackpool. Warbreck Road at this point was very

---

This booklet is reprinted, with additions, from the 1975 and 1976 issues of MODERN TRAMWAY, published monthly by the Light Railway Transport League. Trade distribution by Ian Allan Ltd. For a full list of LRTL books, send SAE to LRTL Publicattions, 13A The Precinct, Broxbourne, Herts E10 7HY.

narrow and the original plan for a single track left no room for a road vehicle to pass on either side of the rails. The Board of Trade therefore advocated what they called double-single line, whereby the two tracks were so close together that trams could not pass each other, but a road vehicle could pass a tram.

At the time the Tramroad was first mooted in 1895, the standard tramway power supply at 500/600v dc could not be efficiently transmitted further than about six miles, because of the resistance of the cables. For longer lines the only practicable solution was to build additional generating stations, and the original plan was to have a power station near each end of the line, one on Ben Sykes' Norbreck Estate at Bispham and the other at Fleetwood, where an expensive site had been bought on the Copse next to the railway line. In 1896 this plan was changed; the site at the Copse would be used instead for an accumulator house, with rows of batteries charged by a direct feeder from the power station at Bispham. Another bank of accumulators would be placed at the Gynn to serve the Blackpool end of the line, and between them the two accumulator houses would provide sufficient power for 100 car-miles, equivalent to six double journeys. It was a mistake, and left the Tramroad Company plagued ever after by the feeble power supply at the Fleetwood end of the line. The site at Copse Road was used for a car shed, but remained under-employed. Building of the Bispham power station was sub-contracted by Dick Kerr to Thomas Riley of Fleetwood, and its 180ft chimney became a local landmark.

John Cameron was appointed General Manager and Secretary of the company, and took up his duties in March 1898. He had been Secretary and General Manager of the Manx Northern Railway since 1879, and had acted as a consultant for the Douglas—Laxey electric line and (since 1895) to the Blackpool and Fleetwood syndicate. He was to wield a most marked influence on the fortunes of the undertaking throughout its independent existence, and so completely did his name become associated with the undertaking that the company's telegraphic address was *"Cameron, Blackpool"*.

Experimental electrical runs on the tramroad section commenced during the last week of June 1898. The first recorded run with passengers from end to end took place on Friday July 1, when members and officials of Blackpool Council and the press were taken from Dickson Road to Fleetwood and back in open-sided car No 4, also visiting the power station at Bispham.

A full description of the line as completed appeared in 'Railway World' for September 1898, to which readers are referred for the complete details, particularly as regards the equipment of the Bispham generating station. The line as completed commenced in Dickson Road opposite Queen Street, from where the leased section of tramway ran with single track along Dickson and Warbreck Roads to the Gynn (pronounced with a hard G), where it met the northern end of the new North Promenade works. There were three passing loops in this section, at Springfield Road, Pleasant Street and Wilton Parade. Double track was laid down the falling gradient from opposite Warley Road down to the Gynn, but the two tracks were too close together to permit cars to pass. From here on, the track was double all the way to the Fleetwood terminus. The grooved rail used in Blackpool weighed 98 lb per yard, the groove being slightly larger than normal to suit the thicker flanges required for running on the Vignoles rails used on the tramroad.

Passing the old Gynn Inn (demolished in 1921), the line crossed on to a sett-paved reservation 330 yards long on the seaward side of a new road (now Queen's Promenade) which had just been laid by the Corporation. This led to the (pre-1918) borough boundary opposite the present King Edward Avenue, where the tramroad proper commenced. At that time, the cliffs rose some 17 feet above the track on the seaward side, these being eventually levelled off and replaced by the sunken gardens. Uncle Tom's Cabin, which gave its name to the first station on the tramroad, was then an old wooden structure standing on the edges of the crumbling cliffs to the west of the track; it became a victim of coast erosion and finally fell into the sea in 1907. A wooden footbridge crossed the line at this point, which, at 95 feet above sea level, was the highest on the whole line.

Continuing along the cliff tops, the line arrived at Bispham, the second station. Here, a single-line spur ran inland for a distance of approximately 400 yards to the generating station, depôt and repair shop. This was also the company's headquarters and main office. Later, this track was opened out to form the present Red Bank Road, now the main shopping street of

Bispham. During its lifetime, the company retained the ownership of Red Bank Road, and on one day each year asserted its lien by closing the road to public traffic by means of a barrier. The depôt adjoined the power station, and had six roads. "Pooldhooie", Mr Cameron's residence, stood nearby and is today the Bispham Conservative Club premises.

From Bispham the tramroad continued on a gradually falling gradient past Norbreck and Little Bispham stations to Anchorsholme. North of Little Bispham the line turned slightly inland through Cleveleys, where there was another station, and was almost level for the remaining distance to Fleetwood. A roadway was built as far as Norbreck by the Gynn and Norbreck Estates Companies soon after the tramroad was opened, and 'Railway World' likened the real-estate boom to those which followed tramway construction in America, the only difference being that there were no maple trees or wooden-framed houses, just sober red brick. A big hydropathic establishment was being built at Norbreck, and the tramroad company was to supply it with current for lighting.

From Cleveleys, a road ran parallel on the west side as far as Rossall, where the line ran close to the famous Rossall School and made a sharp turn before turning north-east; the line at this point was diverted in 1925. There was a halt at Fleetwood Road crossing (now Broadwater) and a second depôt was provided at Copse Road on the outskirts of Fleetwood. Behind this depôt, a physical junction was made with the main line railway sidings. The tramroad section ended at Ash Street, Fleetwood. The Vignoles rails laid on the tramroad were of rather light section, 56 lb per yard, and where spiked direct to creosoted redwood sleepers embedded in 12 inches of ballast. Points and crossovers were of railway pattern. Bispham, Norbreck Cleveleys and Rossall stations were of substantial brick construction and included toilets and waiting rooms; the other stations had simple wooden huts, and all had large railway-type nameboards.

The Fleetwood street section was 1140 yards long via East Street (now Lord Street) and North Albert Street and terminated at the junction with Bold Street. An earlier plan was to continue the line across Bold Street into a field adjoining the North Euston Hotel, where there was to have been an imposing terminal with a turning loop, shops, refreshment and waiting rooms. To minimise disruption Dick Kerr had left the section of line through Fleetwood until last; construction

An official coloured postcard of Blackpool and Fleetwood car 33 sold by the Tramroad Company. The postmark is July 1905. (J. H. Price collection)

began on 7 February 1898 and during the next few weeks the contractor's locomotives became a familiar sight steaming down the street with trainloads of building materials. The Fleetwood street tracks were laid with 83 lb/yd grooved rail and were spaced sufficiently far apart for a cart to stand between.

The overhead wire on the tramroad and in Fleetwood streets was supported on centre poles with double bracket arms. Side bracket arms were used in Dickson and Warbreck Roads, except where the road width necessitated span wires. Decorative scrollwork was confined to the Blackpool and Fleetwood street sections. From the steam-powered Bispham generating station, current was distributed by underground feeder cables laid along the line to cast-iron section boxes placed at half-mile intervals. The accumulator stations were built at the Gynn and at Copse Road, each with a battery of 250 chloride cells; these served to steady the voltage and cope with sudden demands, and supplied the current for the early morning and late night cars.

Above: The original Tramroad track in Lord Street (formerly East Street), Fleetwood in 1920, showing a "Yankee" car of 1899 with its new Blackpool number, 116. The centre-poles remained until the track was relaid and respaced in 1927.
(Courtesy TMS)

Below: Bold Street Tramroad terminus at Fleetwood in company days, with a 28-34 class car. This layout, with its two crossovers, remained in use until the opening of the Ferry loop on May 30 1925.
(Commercial postcard)

Part 2: The Tramroad at work

The Board of Trade inspection, by Major Marindin and Major Cardew, took place on Wednesday July 13 1898. Permission was given for the immediate opening of the portion from the Gynn to Fleetwood, but difficulties arose in Warbreck Road, Blackpool from the fact that the cars were five inches wider than laid down in the Blackpool Tramway Order (1896) and the inspector ruled that the Corporation would have either to widen the road or interlace the tracks. The former alternative was chosen, and the kerbs were set back to give greater clearance, allowing regular service to Dickson Road terminus to commence on September 29.

Public service from the temporary terminus at the Gynn commenced on the day following the inspection, July 14. It far exceeded the Company's highest hopes, and severely taxed the capacities of the ten cars available. 514 000 passengers were carried to September 28, an average of 200 000 per month. To increase the capacity of the service, cars were turned round in as little as 1½ minutes (presumably changing crews); with cars open on both sides it was found possible for 56 passengers to alight and another 56 to board in this time. A formal opening ceremony took place on Saturday July 30, and at Fleetwood the occasion was celebrated as a general holiday.

Construction of a small depôt to hold four cars, together with an office and waiting room at Fleetwood terminus, was begun in October 1898 and completed early in 1899. The double track was continued from the terminus across Bold Street, entering the depôt to give two roads inside. A basic 15-minute service was now established, which continued throughout the company's existence. This was increased to one of about three minutes in the peak holiday season, most of the extra cars starting from the Gynn. The through single fare was sixpence, with intermediate penny stages. Gross receipts between July 14 and December 31 1898 were £12 476, showing a profit of £8584, and an issue of £30 000 of new shares was announced in January 1899, for the purchase of additional rolling stock and generating plant. Plans were also announced for an alternative inland line via Poulton, but this was

Blackpool and Fleetwood
Electric Coast Tramway ...

For a Fare of

6d.

Each Way

For a Fare of

6d.

Each Way

YOU can enjoy an EIGHT-MILE RIDE in luxurious Cars through unrivalled Coast and Country Scenery. A variety of magnificent views- across the Bay of Morecambe to Barrow, and the Mountains beyond, and through a stretch of Beautiful Country teeming with old traditions and old associations.

Visitors should go on the Cars to Fleetwood and see the many sights—the extensive Docks and Shipping, and Fine Promenade.

Cars leave the Gynn and Dickson Road every few minutes in the Summer and every quarter-hour in the Winter— when the cars are heated.

JOHN CAMERON, Manager & Secretary.

opposed by Blackpool Corporation and did not proceed. Additional cars brought the fleet to 34, and additional power plant was installed at Bispham power station early in 1900. The issued capital thereafter remained at its 1900 figure of £150 000, all subsequent expenditure being met from revenue and from the substantial reserves which were steadily accumulated. Typical of the financial operation of the B&FT Company was the half-year ended December 31 1906; total receipts were £23 869 with a surplus of £12 357. This operating ratio of only 44 per cent of the gross earnings was the most favourable in Britain.

The locations selected in 1898 for the two accumulator stations had proved to be less than ideal, and in 1902 the batteries were resited at Bispham and Thornton Gate. During 1903, the capacity of the Blackpool end of the line was increased by lengthening the Wilton Parade loop and inserting an additional passing loop near Warley Road. A lay-by and suitable crossovers were also inserted just north of the Gynn to facilitate the turning of short-working cars from the Fleetwood direction at this point. The extension of Blackpool Corporation's promenade tramway to this point on May 25 1900 had brought many passengers from the South Shore, who could change to the Fleetwood cars at the new terminus. The company was offered the lease of part of the Corporation's new tram shelter at this point for use as an office, but John Cameron demurred at the rent suggested and the Corporation finished up by letting off most of the shelter as a sweet shop.

In February 1899 the Company had ordered 12 cars from the new car works at Preston (six weeks before the works opened), but some months later asked if they could reduce the order by half. The reason was that the Tramroad Company had underestimated the power of the Lancashire & Yorkshire Railway, whose long-standing monopoly of the Blackpool—Fleetwood traffic had taken a severe knock when the Tramroad opened. The railway service was inefficient, since trains had to reverse at Poulton station, often having to wait there for connections. To counter the Tramroad competition, the railway company built a connecting line, the Poulton Curve, which by-passed the station and allowed a direct Blackpool—Fleetwood service. On July 1 1899 they introduced a new service of 19 trains a day in each direction, taking only 15 minutes, and reduced the fare from 9d to 6d, the same as on the Tramroad.

On August 1, the Tramroad company retaliated by introducing a new express service non-stop from the Gynn to Fleet-

Broadwater station (then known as Fleetwood Road crossing) on the Blackpool and Fleetwood Tramroad, looking south. The car, No. 15, is one of the 14-19 series delivered by G. F. Milnes in the autumn of 1898. ('Tramway & Railway World')

A mid-Edwardian scene at the Gynn, with inbound Blackpool and Fleetwood car 20 passing a Blackpool Corporation "Dreadnought" and another Tramroad enclosed car leaving for Fleetwood. The sleeper track commenced at the end of the 300-yard paved reservation in the background.
(Commercial postcard, Advance Series

wood with a special return fare of 10d. This competition with the railway was very beneficial to the passengers, but not too good for the Tramroad Company's accounts, so that the expansion programme had to be curtailed. Nevertheless, the profit earned was still enough for a 10% dividend to be paid on the second half of 1899.

The Tramroad staff had to be prepared to turn their hand to anything. During the height of the summer, the maintenance men and anybody else available would be busy driving trams, whilst in the slack period between Easter and Whit, the summer temporaries would spend time painting the lineside fences, weeding the track and on similar maintenance jobs. Many staff were laid off at the end of the summer season, and a place on the permanent staff was much sought after, particularly as it offered the possibility of renting one of the houses which the company had built for its employees around the Bispham depot. Many men remained on the temporary staff for several summers, and one driver in particular spent each winter working on merchant ships in the China Sea, re-appearing each Easter for a season on the trams.

There was rarely a time when the Tramroad Company was not involved in one legal battle or another. They objected to Bispham Council's charges for making up Queens Drive, they appealed against Fleetwood's charges for constructing Radcliffe Road, and most importantly they set out to prove that the line was not a tramway but a railway, which would bring a 75% reduction in local rates, a potential saving to the Tramroad Company of around £800 a year. The case dragged its way through the local and higher courts between 1903 and 1909, ending up in the House of Lords. By good fortune the unusual title of the line was inconclusive on the matter, and finally the Company came out on top. The victory had a major effect on the income of the local councils, particularly Bispham, where the Tramroad was the largest ratepayer by far.

In 1904, after participating in the Grand Fylde Tour which involved tram to Fleetwood, ferry to Knott End, a horse charabanc to Pilling and the Garstang & Knott End railway, the Tramroad directors floated a new company with John Cameron as manager to operate two Arrol-Johnston motor charabancs between Knott End and Pilling, starting on July 1. By 1907 Fylde Motor Services Ltd had five vehicles running as far afield as Lancaster and Morecambe, and during 1906 they had also run motor launches on the River Wyre, but operations ceased shortly before the railway was extended from Pilling to Knott End on 30 July 1908.

Benjamin Sykes faded from the Tramroad scene after the line was opened, having other problems on his hands, notably the collapse of the Blackpool Alhambra Company in which he lost much of his fortune. Tom Lumb meanwhile was taking over as the main influence on the Fylde coast, having broken away from the firm of Garlick & Sykes in 1900 and set up his own practice as architect, engineer and surveyor. He was still surveyor to the Norbreck Estate and a director of the Cleveleys Hydro, but his most important position as far as the Tramroad was concerned was as managing director of the huge Fleetwood Estate which after mergers now owned the land through which nearly half the Fleetwood Tramroad ran.

Lumb's plans for developing the Fleetwood Estate were centred firmly on the Tramroad. Alongside the line at Rossall Beach he laid out his first new estate, known locally as the Dutch Village from the unusual style of houses which Lumb designed; they can still be seen today opposite Rossall Beach tram stop. He followed this in 1906 by a highly publicised Garden Estate known as Cleveleys Park, which centred on the tram stop which is now Thornton Gate. The Thornton Estate had the right to lay crossings over the line wherever it chose, and Lumb chose to do so much too frequently for the Tramroad's liking. Moreover, the Estate Company wanted the Tramroad to provide tram stops at the new crossings, whereas the Tramroad Company's profits came from whisking carloads of full-fare trippers over the line as fast as the cars could carry them, and not from stopping at street corners on the new estates.

On the other estates further south, the problems were less acute, for the Tramroad served these fairly adequately by short-workings from Talbot Road. Bispham and Cleveleys were natural destinations for many visitors, and in these cases, residential and holiday traffic co-existed fairly happily. The Gynn and Norbreck Estates had, of course, no rights to cross the Tramroad (there would not have been much point) and John Cameron was able to preserve his railway style of operation, with distances of half a mile or more between each Tramroad station. This meant that development tended to be concentrated round the main stations, with the result that Bispham, Norbreck and Cleveleys grew into villages and eventually into sizeable communities in ther own right.

From time to time these growing communities outgrew their own public services. One example was the postal service, which was centred on Preston and gave poor service along the coast. In 1902 the residents of Cleveleys suggested that the mail should be carried along the coast on the Tramroad, and on October 1 1903 the Tramroad introduced its first Postal Cars. An ornate letter box was hung on the back of trams leaving Fleetwood about once every hour through the day, and residents could post letters at any of the Tramroad stations as the car passed through. Each postal car was met at Talbot Road by a GPO official, who took the box to Blackpool post office to catch the next delivery. The new service was very popular with residents, but less so with the company, for at busy stops it delayed the cars, and so the company were not sorry when in 1907 the Post Office agreed to provide proper letter boxes at the stations and empty them during the day in the orthodox manner. The last postal car ran on February 16 1908, but the Tramroad stationmasters were made responsible for emptying the new boxes at 8.30 pm, and mailbags continued to be carried over the Tramroad from Fleetwood.

The outbreak of war in August 1914 found the Tramroad Company on the crest of a wave. Business was booming on the Fylde Coast, culminating in the glorious summer of 1913, when the Tramroad Company carried over 3.6 million passengers and made a profit of £21 000. To cater for the expected increase in traffic, the Company ordered four new trams and extended Bispham depôt. The extension was quite an architectural novelty at the time, being of reinforced concrete built over the reservoir at the back of the shed. It was paid for from the reserve fund, as were the new cars.

During the years up to 1914, the Blackpool and Fleetwood Tramroad Company consistently produced the best financial results of any British tramway. Even during the 1914-18 war, traffic levels continued to be satisfactory, due in part to the large number of service personnel under training in the area. On April 1 1918, the urban district of Bispham-with-Norbreck was amalgamated with the borough of Blackpool, the new boundary being almost at Cleveleys. Blackpool Corporation envisaged extending its Prome-

A side view of a 1-10 series cross-bench car during pre-opening trial runs in 1898. Roof-boards for advertisements were added a year or two later.
('Tramway & Railway World'

nade tram service to Bispham, but it had no powers of compulsory acquisition of the tramroad portion of the B&FT in its new area. The means by which the Corporation eventually bought out the company are described in a later section; agreement was reached during March 1919, and the company agreed to continue operation of the line on behalf of Blackpool Corporation until such time as Parliamentary powers could be obtained for acquisition. Blackpool Corporation guaranteed the ordinary shareholders' dividends at 6½ per cent tax free and retained any profits over and above this amount; the bargain was backdated to January 1 1918, and in that year over £3000 was paid to the Corporation.

The purchase was completed on Wednesday December 31 1919, and Blackpool Corporation took possession on New Year's Day, 1920. The shareholders received about £15 for each £10 share held, a very satisfactory conclusion to a very profitable investment. The Blackpool Improvement Act 1919 which authorised the takeover gave Fleetwood Council the right to purchase the section within its area after 21 years (with the obligation to lease it to Blackpool Corporation for the next 21 years) but this power was not exercised, and the entire tramroad is still owned by Blackpool Corporation.

Part 3: Rolling Stock (i)—The Milnes cars
Fleet list

Blackpool & Fleetwood numbers (to 1919)	Blackpool Corporation numbers (from 1920)	Builder	Type as Built	Seats	Trucks as built	Year
1-10	126-135	G. F. Milnes	Crossbench	48	Milnes	1898
11-13	136-138	G. F. Milnes	Crossbench trailers	48	Milnes	1898
14-19	106-111	G. F. Milnes	6-window Box	48	Milnes	1898
20-24	101-105	G. F. Milnes	8-window Box	48	Milnes	1899
25-27	139-141	G. F. Milnes	Crossbench	48	Milnes	1899
28-34	116-122	ER&TCW	Open "Yankee"	55	Brill 27D	1899
35-37	123-125	UEC	Open "Vanguard"	64	Preston M&G Type	1910
38-41	112-115	UEC	6-window New Box	48	Preston M&G Type	1914

Blackpool and Fleetwood crossbench car 4 in Fleetwood, probably on the pre-opening press trip of July 1 1898. The ten cars of this type maintained the service unaided during the first six weeks of operation from July 14. Livery was brown and ivory. ('Tramway & Railway World'

Dates of withdrawal from passenger service
1924—139; 1926—101; c. 1930—117, 118, 122.
1933—103, 105, 107, 116, 119.
1934—102, 104, 106, 108-111, 120, 121.
1936—112-115.
1937—135, 137, 141.
1938—123-134, 136, 138, 140.

Cars 112, 114, 126, 127, 128, 132, 133, 137, 139 were used subsequently as works cars and snowploughs, and 141 as an illuminated car. Cars 114 and 127 are preserved.

THE original intention of the Tramroad's promoters was that the service would be provided by a fleet of 12 long four-wheel saloon cars and 12 open trailers. 1897 drawings of the original designs have survived, but at the directors' meeting of 7 September 1897 it was decided that all cars should be on bogies. The 1897 drawings show the cars mounted on four-wheel-trucks of the Peckham cantilever type. Successful though it was, the Peckham truck was hardly intended for vehicles 34½ feet long. A car of that length could only run satisfactorily on bogies, and the result was an initial fleet of 24 bogie cars and three bogie trailers, built by G. F. Milnes & Co Ltd of Birkenhead.

Cars 1-10 (Blackpool 126-135) "Old Opens"

The Tramroad Company took delivery of its first car during the Spring of 1898 and put it into use for driver training and testing in May, while the remainder of the class was still under construction at the Milnes works in Birkenhead. It seems that only about five of the others had arrived in time for the opening of the line on July 14 1898, but the entire class of ten was in service shortly afterwards, and proved quite inadequate to meet the demand during the summer when they were the only cars on the line.

The ten cars were of pure American style, open-sided single-deckers with rows of wooden cross bench seats running the full width of the car, so that the conductor had to collect the fares whilst hanging from the side of the car on a long wooden footboard. The controllers were of the latest American General Electric pattern, No K10, and the motors of the newly developed GE1000 type, developing 35 hp. Regrettably, this up-to-date electrical equipment was not matched by the trucks.

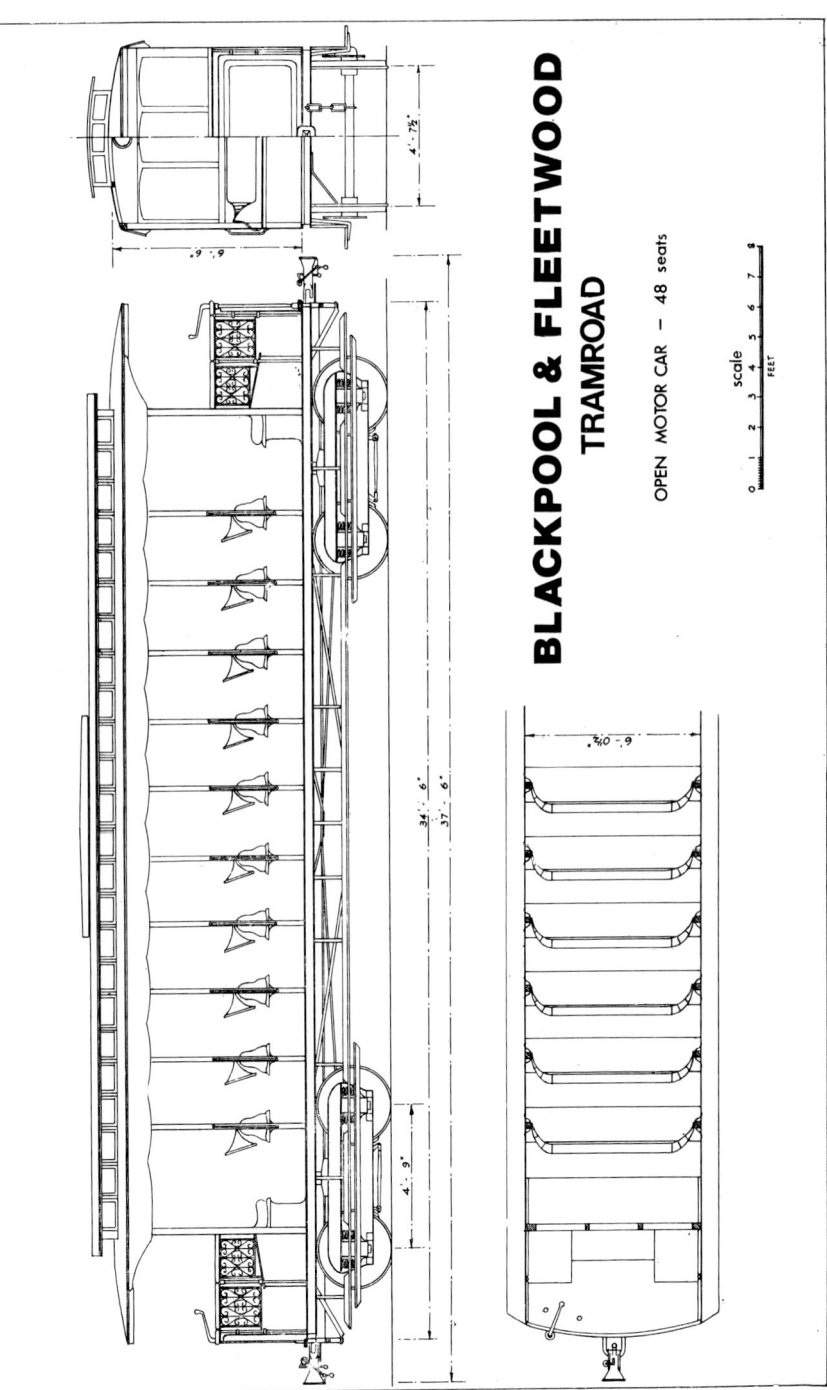

Blackpool Corporation crossbench cars 1-10 of 1898 as built, without lifeguards or headlights and with hinged gates to the platforms, which carried only sand and tool boxes instead of a seat.

Blackpool Corporation 136, a motored Tramroad trailer, as running in 1931. The three trailers were built without end platforms, and resembled those on the MER; they were withdrawn by 1902, and after five years in store were converted to motor trams. This involved extending the underframes (the "patch" is visible in the photograph), adding driving platforms and canopies, and mounting the cars on Mountain & Gibson motor bogies. Seats were provided on the platforms, increasing the capacity to 56. (M. J. O'Connor)

These followed Isle of Man practice, being of plate frame type set right at the ends of the body. By 1898 there were several more modern bogies available, and 'Railway World' commented: *"The trucks do not impress one as being equal to the best American types. These may cost rather more, but it is poor economy to retrench in this particular, as the life of the car body is so largely dependent on the character of the trucks".*

Photographs exist of cars 2, 3, 4, 5 and 9 as identical open-sided crossbench cars, and cars 1-10 can safely be assumed to have been identical. However, the maker's drawing shows that they seated only 48 and not, as had been thought, 56 since the driver's platforms were not originally fitted with seats. The very similar Manx Electric cars 14-18 had platform seats as built, but perhaps the Board of Trade, who had no jurisdiction in the Isle of Man, frowned on their use; there were sand- and tool-boxes on the platforms and people did sometimes sit on them, but the platform seats were not made official until some years later. The tool-box also served (and still serves at Crich on car 2) as a locker for the ticket-box and for overcoats, etc.

Cars 11-13 (Blackpool 136-138) "Trailers"

These three cars have always been something of a mystery. Their existence was known (mainly from the statistics), but no photographs or drawings have ever been discovered to indicate exactly what they were like when built, or how they were numbered. It is necessary therefore to resort to some detective work.

Firstly, as regards the numbers, we have seen that cars 1-10 were in service by August 1898, and we now have evidence that the trailers were in use by the beginning of September. On August 26 the company chairman had reported that they had only ten cars, but that two covered cars and three trailers were expected within eight days, and on September 2 a girl was injured at Fleetwood terminus hitching a ride "whilst a car was being shunted". Furthermore, 'Tramway & Railway World' for August 1898 confirms that the original rolling stock order included three trailers. Since we know that the first covered "Box" car went into service in mid-September 1898 and that "Box" car 15 was running by September 28, it seems fairly certain that the first two enclosed cars to arrive were 14 and 15, and that the three trailers were 11-13. This supposition is borne out by the recent discovery of a commercial postcard showing a motored trailer car bearing the number 13.

The second reassessment concerns the vehicles themselves. There are such obvious similarities between the open and closed motor cars of the Fleetwood Tramroad and those of the Manx Electric Railway that one would expect to find a corresponding link in the case of the trailers, and that the Fleetwood trailers, like the MER trailers of various designs, had been built without platforms. These sus-

Blackpool & Fleetwood crossbench cars 3 and 13 passing at the Gynn, probably about 1907. This photograph provided final confirmation of the author's reassessment of the tramroad's rolling stock, for No 13 with its angular canopy is clearly one of the three motored trailers which became Blackpool Corporation 136-138.
(Real Photograph Series

picions now have some fairly substantial backing following the discovery of a Mather and Platt drawing dated August 20 1897, which shows a four-wheel open trailer intended for the Fleetwood Company. This car has thirteen portals, as has car 136 in the facing photograph, and its dimensions tally almost exactly with those of the main body of motored trailer cars. As we shall see when we come to the Box cars, the four-wheel truck must have been replaced by bogies before the design was finished.

It had been thought that the design of the Fleetwood trailers might be similar to the 1899 Manx Electric cars. But in fact the car in the drawing is of a wider, longer (by one bench) version of the 1894 Milnes MER trailers, of which No 36 and 37 survive today. The Fleetwood car seats 48 passengers on twelve benches, leaving the ends free for the double brake wheels which can be seen today on the MER cars. The end bulkheads are glazed and gracefully curved, with a central droplight, and the gently arched roof is supported by six pillars spaced rather differently from the Manx cars because of the extra seat.

So far, unfortunately, no photographs of the trailers as such have come to light, and there seems little chance of any views existing of the cars in service, since their career as trailers was very brief. We know that they were running in 1899 by an illuminating report of an accident on August 21: *"Soon after 6 o'clock a car with trailer attached was passing the Norbreck crossing on its way to Fleetwood and immediately behind it was an open car in charge of a man named Mason. The front car, unknown to Mason, was brought to a standstill and when he became aware of the fact he was within six yards of the trailer. He endeavoured to stop the car by applying the emergency brake but the distance was too short and the car dashed into the trailer, pitching it off the line and slightly damaging the front and the windows."*

It must have become obvious very soon that trailer operation, however practicable on the MER with its reserved-track layout was both inconvenient and dangerous in the disorganised conditions which prevailed in busy times at the Tramroad's street-track terminals. There is no evidence that Blackpool or Fleetwood

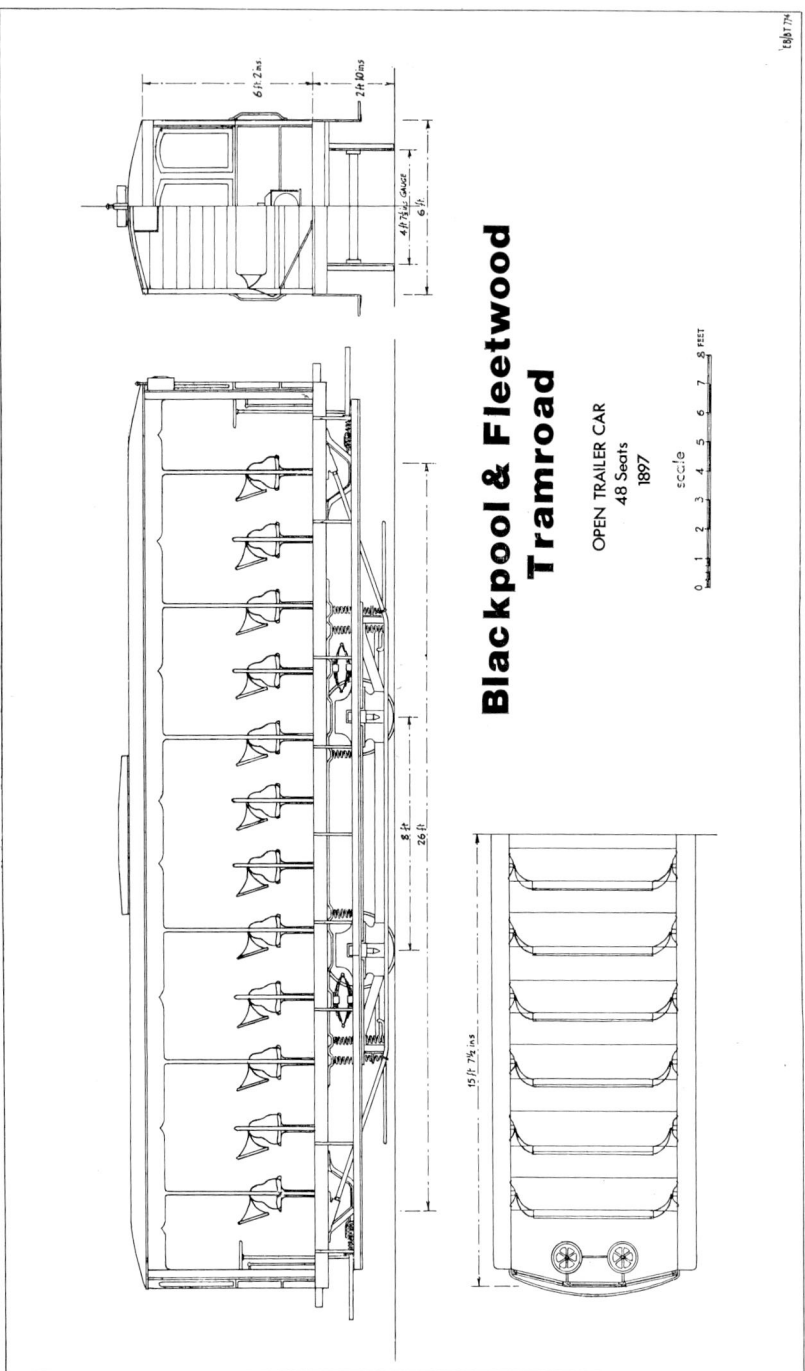

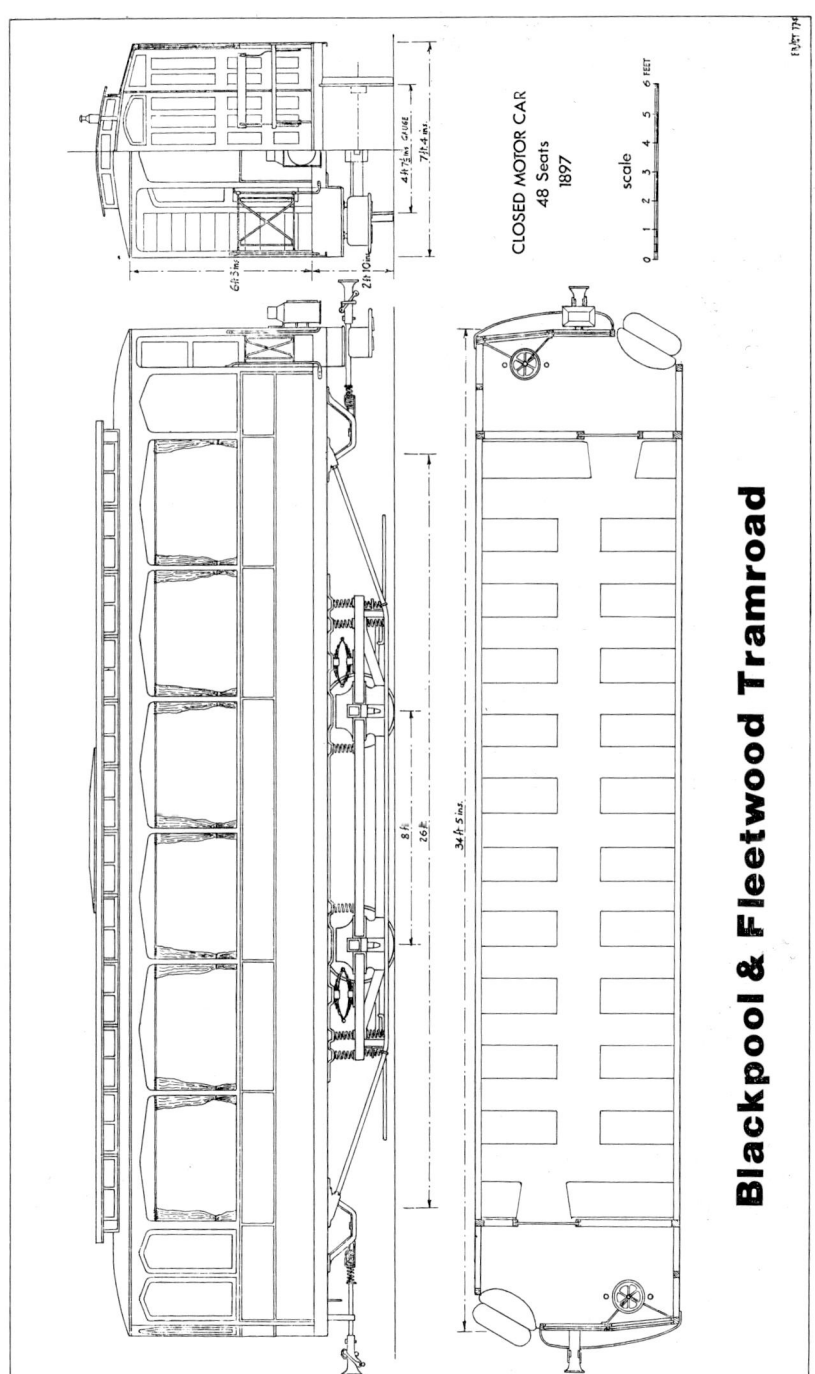

Councils raised any objections, but the Board of Trade, never the greatest proponent of trailer operation, presumably did. It seems that at one time the company had intended to make trailer operation a regular feature, an eventual fleet of 30 motors and 30 trailers being mentioned in the press, but these plans were soon abandoned.

By 1902, only 31 of the 34 cars were relicensed, and three years later the Chairman reported that the trailers could not be used in Blackpool or Fleetwood, something of a limitation for a line which served only a handful of houses between the two towns. Shortly afterwards the three cars were motored, presumably having to be sent to the closely associated Strand Road works at Preston, since the rebuilding was considerable. A new clerestory roof, new platforms and Mountain and Gibson bogies gave the rebuilt cars such an impressive appearance that according to Mr Donald Cameron, son of the Manager, they were nicknamed "Powerful", "Dreadnought" and "Dreadful".

Cars 14-24 (Blackpool 101-111) "Box Cars"

These cars fall into two classes, six-window and eight-window. The first to arrive were six-window cars 14-19 in the autumn of 1898, and these were followed about six months later by eight-window cars 20-24. From 1920, cars 14-19 ran as Blackpool 106-111 whilst 20-40 took the Blackpool numbers 101-105.

We know that car 15 was running by September 1898 and car 18 by November and we can confidently date the entire batch of six-window cars to 1898. Electric heaters were installed in one of these cars during December 1898 and are believed to have been extended to the other six-window cars soon afterwards. It would appear that in the early years these cars were used for the basic winter service, since every accident which was reported during the close season involved a car of the 14-19 class.

The second batch of Box cars, 20-24, arrived from Milnes around Easter 1899. These five cars are very interesting in that the bodies were virtual facsimiles of the famous Manx Electric saloons 19-22 which survive to this day. They had the same eight drop-windows in the saloon, a marked improvement on the six-window 14-19 class which relied entirely on the clerestory for ventilation. The drop-windows must have been much appreciated by passengers in summer, though not by a lady whose son's hat blew out of the window of car 23 whilst travelling into town alongside Dickson Road. On descending from the car to retrieve the hat the unfortunate lady was distressed to hear the guard ring the bell and see the car — and child — disappearing down the road. So distressed was she, in fact,

Blackpool & Fleetwood six-window box car 19 at Cleveleys, about 1900. The six cars of this type (14-19) were built by G. F. Milnes in 1898. (courtesy R. B. Parr

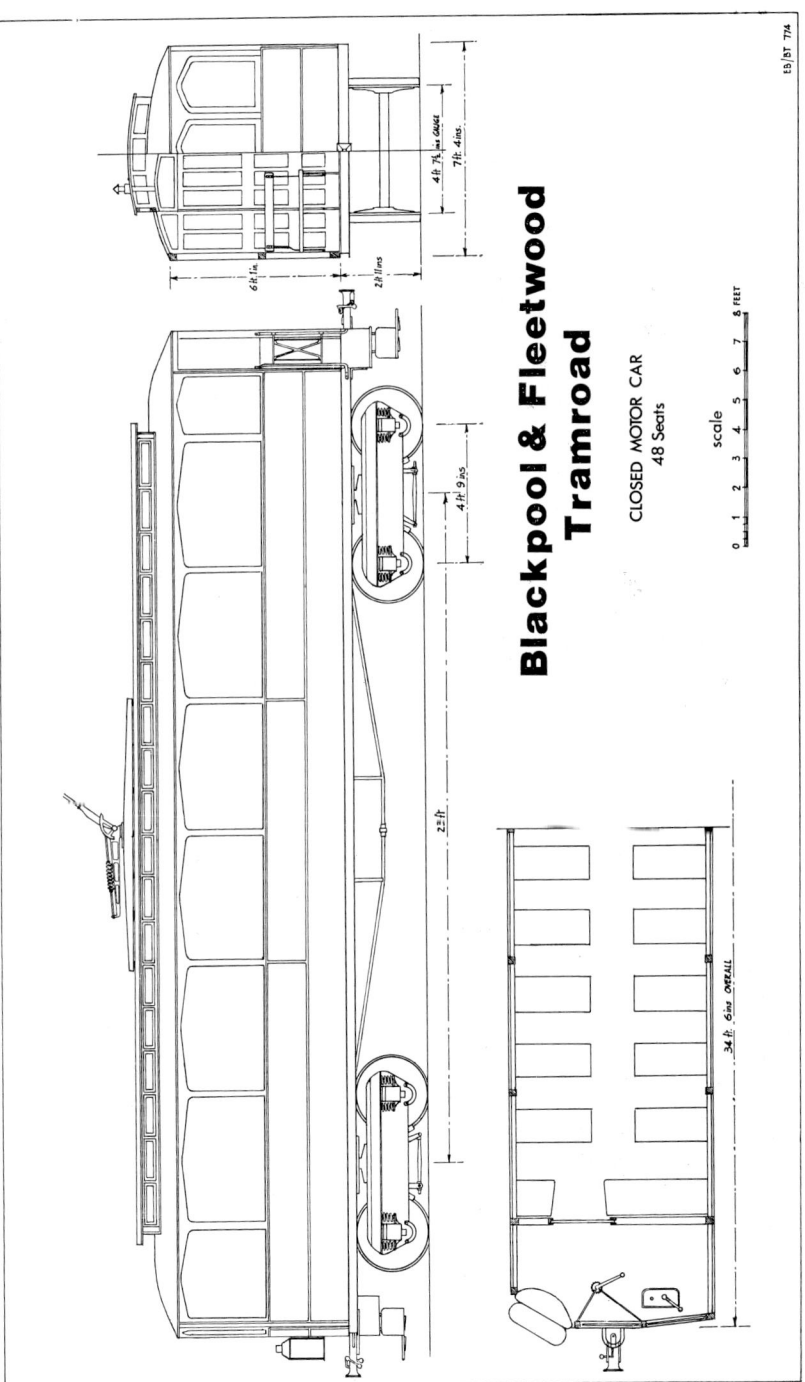

Blackpool & Fleetwood Tramroad

CLOSED MOTOR CAR
48 Seats

A drawing traced from a Milnes original of Blackpool & Fleetwood six-window "Box" cars 14-19 of 1898. Slight changes were made during construction, such as the substitution of plain arch for tudor-arch windows and dividing the offside platform window. These cars were the mainstay of the winter service in company days; they became Blackpool Corporation 106-111.

Eight-window Box car 24 in East Street, Fleetwood. These cars (Blackpool & Fleetwood 20-24) were generally similar to Manx Electric winter saloons 19-22. East Street was renamed Lord Street in 1911. (Courtesy C. Carter

that she reported the affair to the 'Gazette-News', which is how we come to know the sad tale.

The electric heating of the Box cars was improved in 1901 and at the same time the saloons were divided by a partition into smoking and non-smoking compartments, a concession to public comfort which was not altogether typical of the Tramroad Company.

Like the crossbench motor cars, the Box cars had Milnes plate-frame bogies set right at the ends of the vehicle with a distance between bogie centres of 23 feet, only practicable on lines like the Tramroad and the MER which had no tight curves on the public highway. They were 34 feet 6 inches long, and it seems inconceivable that they should have been designed originally as four-wheelers. Nevertheless there exists a Mather & Platt drawing which shows a car body of exactly the same dimensions as the six-window Box cars 14-19 (though with Tudor arch instead of round arch windows) mounted on an 8-foot wheelbase Peckham cantilever truck. On the drawing is written by hand *"Produced at Directors' Meeting 7th September 1897. These plans superse'd by others suggested by Mr Parry, 13th October 1897."* A similar drawing of a four-wheeled crossbench trailer survives with the same message written on it, and there was probably an equivalent four-wheel design for the crossbench motor cars. Mr Parry's suggestion was presumably for bogie cars, since a Milnes drawing shows a virtually identical body mounted on plate-frame bogies and this, apart from window detail, represents a car of the 14-19 class.

Both the Mather & Platt and the Milnes drawings show the six-window cars quite bereft of lifeguards despite the fact that they were to run on the public highway, and it was in this form that they entered service. What the Board of Trade thought about it, if indeed they knew, would be illuminating, especially as the crossbench cars had by this time been fitted with lifeguards and had run the service without serious incident for the first two months.

The new Box cars, with their murderous bogies mounted quite nakedly at the extremities of the car, soon altered that. Car 15 had only been in service for a week or so when, on September 27 1898, it ran down an 84-year-old man outside St Peter's Church at Fleetwood. It was the Tramroad's first fatality. The next was not long coming, for on November 15 Box car 18 recorded victim No 2 at Bispham, and five weeks later crossbench car 3 added another by killing a pedestrian at Uncle Tom's Cabin while carrying a load of fire bars. Not for nothing did the local press refer to the Tramroad as "the slaughterhouse line".

Shortly afterwards the Box cars were fitted with lifeguards and the carnage diminished somewhat, though in those days of primitive surgery anybody coming into contact with a Tramroad car travelling at anything like its normal speed had little chance of survival, lifeguard or not. The early days of the company are recorded in a succession of gruesome inquest reports which, though regrettable, have been of great value in the preparation of this history.

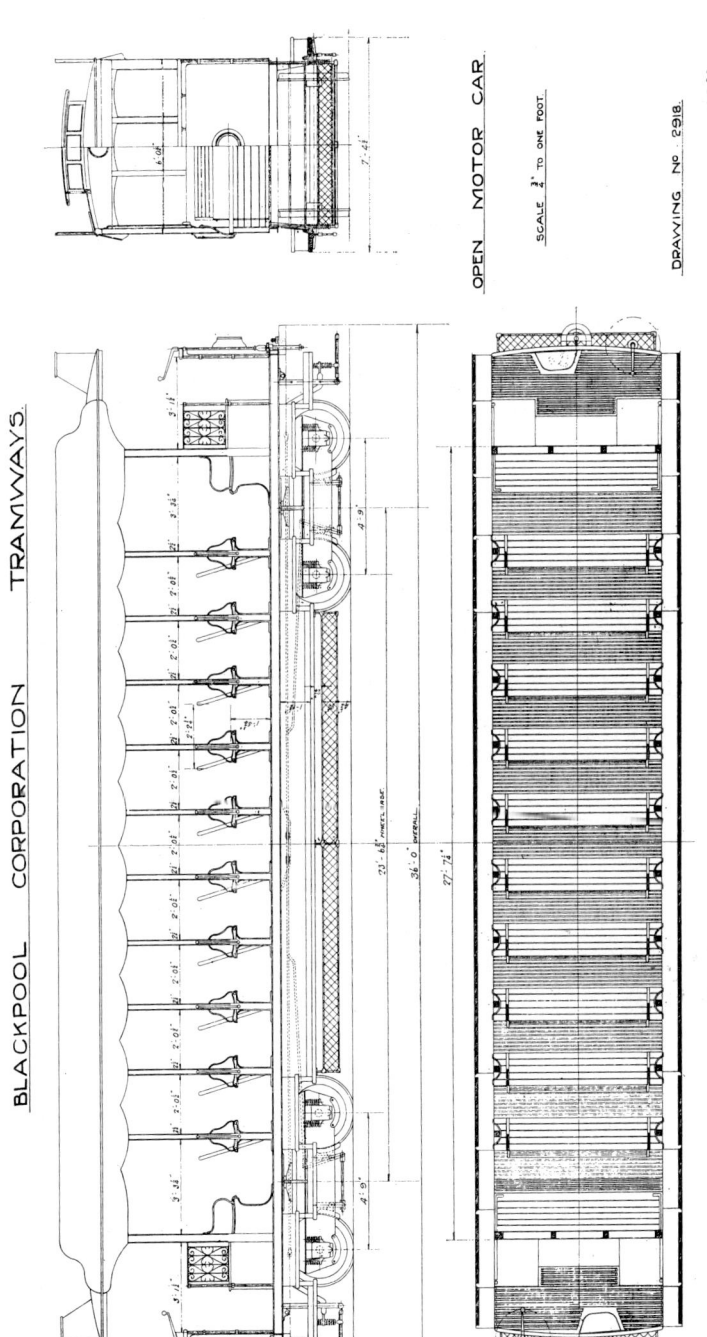

A Blackpool Corporation drawing of the 139-141 crossbench series, built in 1899 by G. F. Milnes as Blackpool & Fleetwood Tramroad 25-27, shown as running in 1929. The 1898 crossbench cars 1-10 (Blackpool 126-135) were generally similar.

Cars 25-27 (Blackpool 139-141) "Old Opens"

In a previously published fleet list these three cars were listed as 11-13, part of the original class of 13 crossbench cars which eventually became Blackpool 126-135 and 139-141. There are several reasons for doubting this.

Firstly the odd gap in the Blackpool numbering suggests that these three did not belong to the same batch as cars 1-10. Secondly the evidence outlined earlier suggests very strongly that cars 11-13 were in fact the trailers. And thirdly, car 25, described as a trailer in the previously-mentioned list, was twice involved in accidents during 1899 and on both occasions was described as an "open car" in contexts which make it clear that it could not possibly have been a trailer.

In February 1899, the Chairman had announced that new cars were expected during March or April and that the fleet would then total 27. It seems fairly certain that these three cars were delivered at this time and took the numbers 25-27 after the second batch of Box cars, cars 20-24, which were probably included in the same delivery from Milnes. The new cars were almost identical to the 1-10 class, but examination of photographs of Blackpool 139 and 141 reveals detailed differences in the clerestory ends and the position of the controller. In the absence of photographs of company cars 25-27, we cannot be absolutely certain that this hypothesis is correct and we would be particularly glad to hear from any reader who knows of photographs of these elusive cars.

Delivery of cars 20-27 by Easter 1899 completed the Tramroad Company's initial rolling stock purchases in time for the first full season of operation. The new fleet of 11 saloons, 13 crossbench motor cars and 3 trailers typified the Tramroad Company's eminently practical approach, as they established what was to prove one of the most efficient and profitable privately-owned tramways in Great Britain. The new cars represented no technological advance; indeed, even at that early date, they could be regarded as slightly old-fashioned. They were direct cousins of cars which had been proved on the closely associated Manx Electric Railway, built, probably from the same drawings, by G. F. Milnes of Birkenhead as sub-contractors to Mather & Platt, main contractors for both lines.

These 27 cars were the last to be bought from "outside" builders. The company's future requirements would naturally be supplied by the new car

Staff and cars of the Blackpool & Fleetwood Tramroad pose for a local viewcard publisher at Bispham station, probably in 1903. On the left is a Preston-built car of the 28-34 class, showing the storm blinds and the wire mesh which enclosed the knifeboard seats at each end; on the right, heading for Blackpool, is Milnes Box car 16. (Commercial postcard

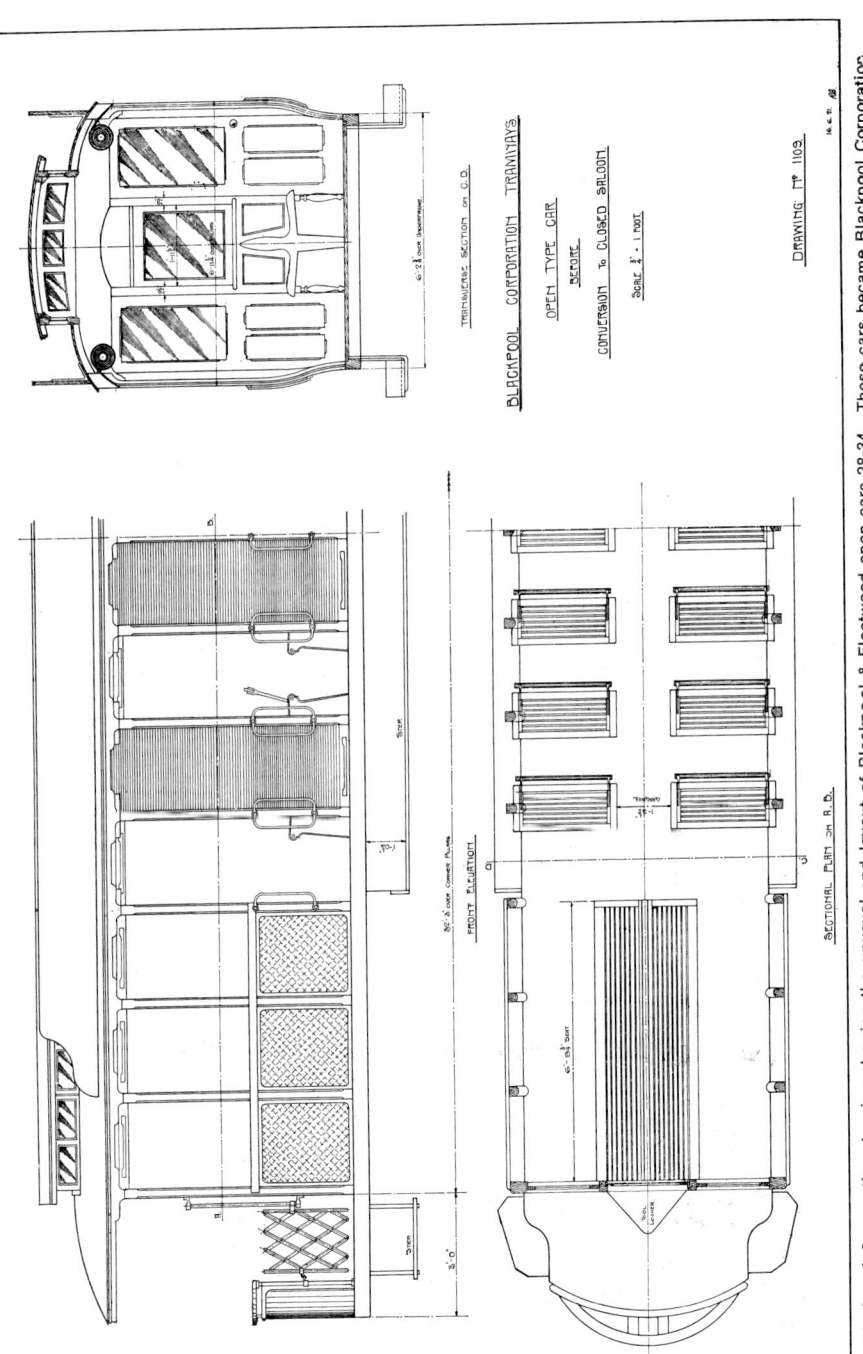

A Blackpool Corporation drawing showing the unusual end layout of Blackpool & Fleetwood open cars 28-34. These cars became Blackpool Corporation 116-122, and most were rebuilt in the early 1920's as enclosed saloons known unofficially as Glasshouses. The roller shutters were added in 1907, and the seats were divided by a gangway in 1917 to assist wartime lady conductors.

works which was being built at Strand Road, Preston, by the same hard-headed directors who had guided the Fleetwood Tramroad to its highly successful opening. In the later parts of this article we shall discuss the vehicles which arrived from this new works over the next fifteen years, and see how they and the earlier cars were eventually incorporated into the Blackpool Corporation fleet.

Part 4: Rolling Stock (ii)—The Preston cars

THE first 27 cars of the Blackpool & Fleetwood Tramroad Company had all been built by G. F. Milnes & Company of Birkenhead, and all had strong Manx Electric antecedents. In 1899, however, the Electric Railway & Tramway Carriage Works Ltd, closely associated with the Blackpool & Fleetwood Company, opened its doors at Strand Road, Preston. Over the next 15 years, this new works was to produce the remainder of the Tramroad Company's fleet, cars 28 to 41.

Cars 28-34 (Blackpool 116-122) "Yankees"

Of all the distinctive cars operated by the Blackpool & Fleetwood Tramroad Company, these seven open bogie cars are the most intriguing. They had a strange, almost unique, seating arrangement whereby a central crossbench section was flanked by semi-enclosed knifeboard seats; this was probably adopted to keep within the limits of width which the earlier cars had been criticised for exceeding. According to the Chairman they were "of an American type", which seems a rather confusing statement since the original crossbench cars were far more transatlantic in appearance. Nevertheless, the label stuck, to such good effect that the belief was held very strongly in Corporation days that the cars had been built in the USA and shipped over in knocked-down state.

The Blackpool Times, however, reported on Sept 20 1899 that "the new Fleetwood tramcars, which are of the American type, will probably be brought into use this weekend. Two of them arrived at the Fleetwood car shed on Sunday morning (17th), having come direct on their own wheels on the railway from Preston. The cars, which have been manufactured by the Preston Electric Carriage Works . . . are capable of holding 55 passengers." These may well have been the first Preston-built electric cars to enter service anywhere and some of the very few to be delivered on their own wheels—only possible because of their deep flanges and the railway link at Copse Road.

A builder's photograph of the Blackpool & Fleetwood 28-34 class as built in 1900, showing the unusual end layout and the Brill 27D trucks. (United Electric Car Company.)

The bogies of the 28-34 class were most unusual, being Brill 27D's, a design so rare in this country that the only other known examples were under the ER&TCW yard crane at Strand Road. The 27D, an 1897 predecessor of the popular 27G, was not at all common even in its native USA. Perhaps they were obtained by the ER&TCW from Brill cheaply, as a discontinued line; the design was already slightly out of date, and it is hardly likely that the Tramroad Company specified that particular bogie. However, they served at Blackpool until the 1920's.

Only the bogies were built at Preston. Controllers (Type S7) and motors (44S) were from Walkers of Ohio, and the trolley base was the distinctive Union Standard No. 5, made by Nuttall's of Pittsburgh, which was standard on the Tramroad fleet but used nowhere else in Britain. The bogies likewise bore prominent "Brill, Philadelphia" maker's plates, which helped foster the "Yankee" notion. The fitting of air-brakes (American, of course) also contributed to the trans-Atlantic image.

The Tramroad's original order was for six cars, the seventh being built by ER&TCW for display at the 1900 Tramways Exhibition at the Agricultural Hall, Islington and purchased later. This is borne out by the recollection of one old employee that one of the "Yankees" had silver-plated commode handles. The subsequent history and rebuilding of some of these cars after 1920 will be dealt with in a later instalment.

Cars 35-37 (Blackpool 123-125) "Vanguards"

The Fleetwood Tramroad was unusual among British electric tramways in that it bought not a single new car during the great "boom" period between 1900 and 1910. When at last new trams did arrive in August 1910, they proved to be the ultimate British development of the roofed crossbench single-decker and, as it turned out, the last open cars to be bought by the company. Known to the staff somewhat inappropriately as "Vanguards", a name of probably naval inspiration, they followed the same basic design as the rebuilt trailer cars 11-13, but with the added refinement of driver's windscreens. These screens had five windows, the outer panes being very narrow and giving a wrap-round effect.

Although windscreens on open cars were not unknown in America, particularly on the faster-running lines, they were unusual in Britain. Indeed screens of any sort were rare on the crowded Fylde coast tramways, where rear-end collisions were too frequent for comfort in the days before safety-glass was perfected and air brakes became common. Nearly 20 years were to pass before Blackpool Corporation started to fit screens even to its closed cars. In the case of Tramroad cars 35-37, the provision of windscreens may have been a condition imposed by the company's evident wish to add passenger seats on the platforms, by

A builder's photograph of Blackpool & Fleetwood 37, one of the three Vanguard class cars (35-37) which later became Blackpool 123-125. These cars were fitted as new with platform seats, windscreens and roller shutters. (United Electric Car Company)

Blackpool Corporation's ex-conduit engineering car 4 standing on Tramroad company tracks at the Gynn, during the period from 1913 to 1915. The Corporation owned and maintained this section of track, and although the tracks were not joined to the Promenade tramway the engineering car was evidently manhandled across the gap as necessary.
(Courtesy TMS

which they achieved in these cars the respectable capacity of 64 persons.

The "Vanguards" did at least merit their nickname in one respect; they were the first new cars on the Fylde coast to be mounted on Preston swing-bolster bogies —officially "No 27 PC2 Light Type"— which from 1911 until 1929 became the standard bogie for all new Tramroad and Corporation cars. By 1930 these bogies, a derivative of the former Mountain & Gibson No 9 design, were fitted to some 120 out of a total of 157 trams in the Blackpool fleet.

Cars 38-41 (Blackpool 112-115) "New Boxes"

The final additions to the Company stock in 1914 were a disappointment in view of the gradual development which had taken place in tramcar design since 1898. They were almost identical in body design to the 14-19 batch of 1898, except that the clerestory was omitted and opening quarter-lights fitted for ventilation. The retention of the difficult and restricted corner entrance (a Milnes feature inherited from steam tramways)

A builder's picture of the first of the four U.E.C.-built saloon cars ("New Box" class, cars 38-41) as delivered in 1914. Apart from the trucks, these cars were built to what was virtually an 1898 design. (United Electric Car Company

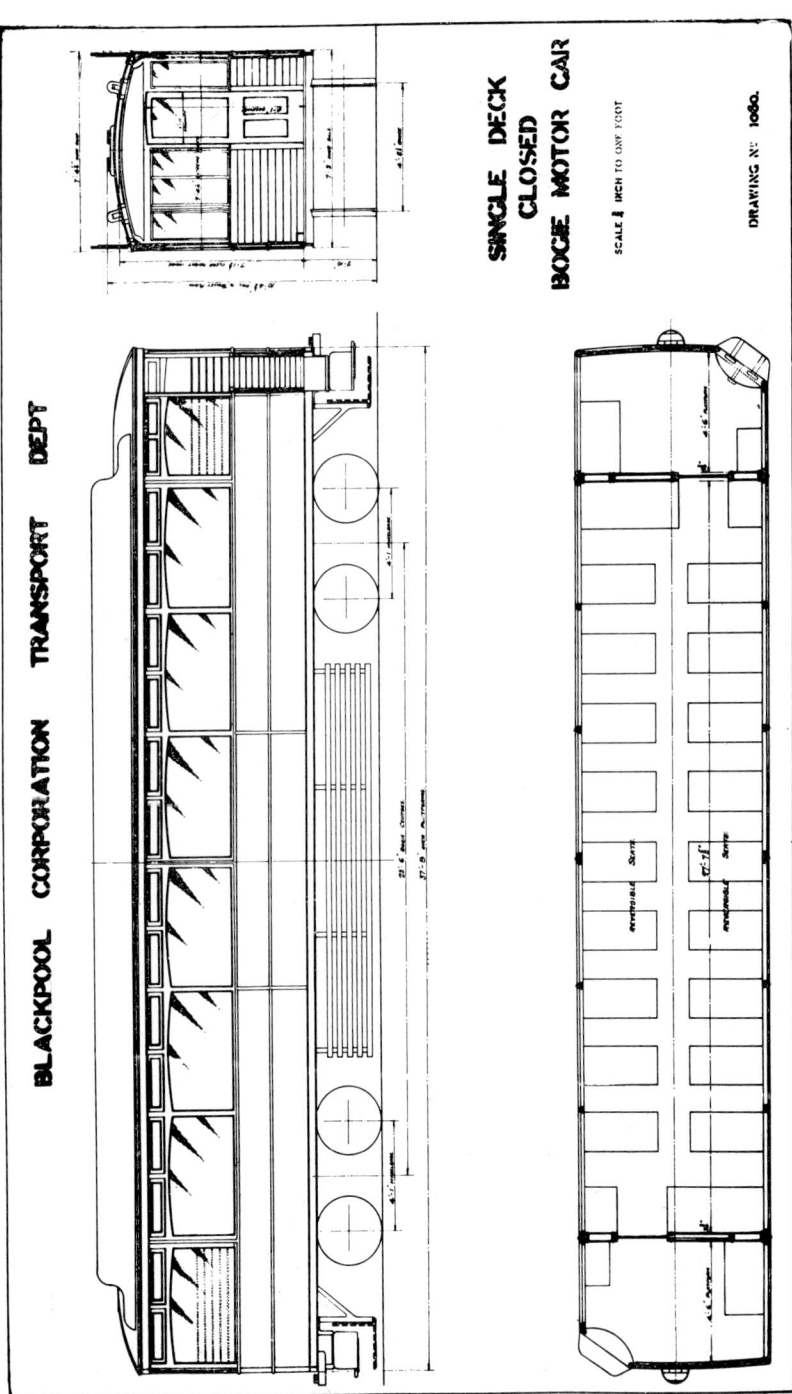

A Blackpool Corporation drawing of the last cars to be built for the Tramroad company (38-41, later Blackpool 112-115). No major alterations were made to these cars by the Corporation; one of them (114) became a works car in 1937 and has been preserved.

showed a lack of understanding of the changing nature of the tramroad, as the open fields between the two towns began to fill with houses. It seems odd that such an archaic design should have been commissioned from a builder who had not constructed the originals, when a more modern car could just as easily have been produced. Odd, too, that the Company should have wanted to buy new trams when their lease in Blackpool had only five more years to run. It was a measure of the Tramroad's financial standing that these new cars were paid for out of revenue.

Other vehicles, built or proposed

We have now considered all 41 of the Tramroad Company's passenger cars. Before going on to study their subsequent history as part of the Blackpool Corporation fleet, we must pause for a moment and discuss two other types of vehicle which graced the Tramroad in its independent days.

Double-deckers

No double-deck passenger cars ever ran on the Tramroad in company days, and the Board of Trade would even then have frowned upon the use of such cars on open track without check rails. It is all the more surprising, therefore, that amongst the cache of Tramroad drawings recently discovered should be a Dick Kerr drawing, undated, of a five-window maximum traction open-top bogie car, a shorter version of a type supplied in 1898-9 to Blackburn Corporation and the Imperial Tramway Company at Middlesbrough. It appears to be a standard Dick Kerr drawing on which Blackpool & Fleetwood Tramroad lettering has been added and, though its chances of acceptance seem slim, it must have been part of a serious bid by Dick Kerr to obtain the Blackpool & Fleetwood electrical contract which eventually went to Mather & Platt, who subcontracted the cars to G. F. Milnes.

Although double-deckers never ran on the Tramroad in passenger service, they did run on other occasions. On October 16-17 1903, five of the Blackpool St Annes & Lytham company's new open-top cars were dragged across the gap between Corporation and company tracks at the Gynn to spend the winter in Copse Road depôt, the new Squires Gate depôt being not yet completed. They returned on May 16 1904.

A photograph exists, too, of Blackpool's ex-conduit engineering car 4 (now preserved) standing on the Company's third track at the Gynn some time between 1913 and 1915. The Corporation owned and maintained this section of the Company's route, and presumably were not averse to manhandling the little engineering car across the gap.

Locomotives

Little information has come to light, during the present researches, on the steam locomotives which were used by Dick Kerr, the contractors for the permanent way. At least two engines were operating on the line, since a report appeared in the 'Gazette-News' of a journey from Blackpool to Fleetwood in 17 minutes by "one of the steam engines now in use" on March 11 1898. It is possible that the locomotives remained on the line after construction, since a legal settlement reported in 'Tramway and Railway World' for August 8 1901 reveals that twelve ballast wagons had been hired from T. N. Brown (contractor) of Leeds in 1899 by the Tramroad Company itself.

The only recorded occasion when passengers were officially conveyed by steam train occurred on March 13 1898, when a special journey was made for the press. It is perhaps worth quoting the 'Gazette-News' report:

... by about 2.15 a party of seven—lucky number—were comfortably seated on chairs placed in a waggon to be drawn by an engine called the 'Fleetwood'. It was not exactly an up-to-date corridor train, and although the wind blew in pretty piercing blasts we were quite comfortable deep down in the Pullman car. We left Fleetwood amid affectionate leave-takings and were soon well in sight of good old Rossall. Rapidly we steamed through fields, crossed bridges and skimmed between budding hedgerows and in the short space of twenty minutes we were actually in breezy Blackpool. After a look round Blackpool we started our homeward journey, this being a little before five, and after a few stoppages just to give the engine breathing space—not in order to satisfy any desire of our own—we were at home ready for Church, having spent a Pleasant Sunday Afternoon."

According to surviving Preston works records, the Tramroad Company placed an order in 1900 for four motors and two controllers to equip an electric locomotive. No evidence survives to prove that this vehicle was built or delivered. It had been thought that a locomotive might well have been used to haul coal wagons from exchange sidings at Copse Road, Fleetwood, to the power station at Bispham depôt, but one of John Cameron's sons recalled that wagons of coal for the power station were always pulled by the normal crossbench cars which served as works cars during the winter. At other times, coal was brought by cart from Layton railway station.

Although the 1897 prospectus stated that the connection at Fleetwood would enable the company to obtain its coal cheaply from the Wigan coalfield, it appears that in later years Blackpool Corporation entertained doubts about the legal status of the facility, and found it advisable to obtain its own separate authorisation. Powers to construct a siding were granted in the Blackpool Improvement Bill of 1920, which also empowered the Corporation to carry goods and minerals over the Tramroad. These powers were exercised from 1927 to 1949, and details appear in a later section of this history. Since the tramroad fleet did not include a locomotive, the Corporation ordered a new one themselves.

Part 5: The Corporation takes over

ON Wednesday, December 31 1919, at the Talbot Road offices of the Manchester & Liverpool District Bank, the Borough Treasurer of Blackpool handed to Mr John Cameron, General Manager of the Blackpool & Fleetwood Tramroad Company, a cheque for £297 758:7:1, and the Corporation became the owners of seven miles of tramroad, a power station, three depôts and 41 tramcars. The company retained its investment fund of £42 052 and repaid its shareholders at the rate of £15 for each £10 share.

This was the last act in a rather bizarre sequence of events which had begun during the First World War when Blackpool made it clear that they would not renew the company's lease within the Borough when it expired in 1919. The Corporation, concerned at the fact that many of the resort's attractions lay beyond the borough boundary and outside their control, were determined to extend their influence to the whole Fylde coast. They were particularly concerned at the precarious condition of the popular cliffs at Bispham, where the coastline was being eroded at such a rate that the tramroad itself would eventually fall into the sea.

Bispham Council had no resources to combat the erosion and so, on April 1 1918, Blackpool Corporation absorbed Bispham-with-Norbreck and immediately began pouring large sums of money into a scheme of sea-defences to save the crumbling cliff face. This enlargement of the borough meant that almost half the Fleetwood tramroad was now in Corporation territory, and it placed the Tramroad Company in an even more invidious position.

Before the war, the Company had formulated a scheme for an alternative entry into Blackpool, and had reached the stage of preparing Parliamentary plans, before the war brought matters to a halt. Just where this new approach was to be made is not known, but it may well have involved co-operation with the railway companies, possibly by a link to Bispham (now Layton) station and an entry over the railway to Talbot Road. A similar arrangement could have been planned at Fleetwood.

The railways were certainly very interested in the Blackpool & Fleetwood Tramroad, serving, as it did, a rapidly growing residential and holiday area between the two towns. Ever since its opening in 1898 the tramroad had been a thorn in their flesh, defying all the competition which the Lancashire and Yorkshire company could devise in the way of direct Blackpool—Fleetwood trains, reduced running times, higher frequencies and bargain fares. Matters came to a head in July 1918 when a whisper was heard in "informed circles" that the Lancashire and Yorkshire Railway Company was about to make an offer for the Fleetwood tramroad. It was a very quiet whisper, but it did reach the ears of the Mayor of Blackpool, and that was enough. For at that time Blackpool had as mayor perhaps the ablest man ever to fill the post, before or since—Alderman Albert Lindsay Parkinson, founder of the famous construction company which bears his name, and already a man of considerable personal fortune.

Lindsay Parkinson was not a man to let the grass grow under his feet; the 'Blackpool Times' described him as *"a superman, doubly-endowed with foresight, accustomed to swiftness of decision and lightning-like rapidity of action".* The Mayor certainly lived up to this reputation for, within a week, without saying a word to any member of the Corporation, he had bought the tramroad. On July 17 1918, Lindsay Parkinson called together the senior members of the Town Council and told them, to their astonishment, that he had obtained options on sufficient tramroad shares to secure control of the company, and was prepared for the Corporation to take over these options at no profit to himself. If they were not interested, he would be obliged to sell to "another company".

At any other time and place, Lindsay Parkinson's disregard for the niceties of democratic local government might have been ill received. In wartime Blackpool, though, the coup was received by the Council with great satisfaction. The Corporation rapidly concluded an agreement to purchase the company, and set about preparing a Parliamentary Bill to authorise the take-over and the construction of tramways to join the two systems. It was thought to be only a matter of time before the Corporation absorbed the Blackpool St Annes and Lytham Tramway Company, thereby realising the Council's ambition of a unified tramway system for the entire coast and, on November 4 1918, approval was given for Charles Furness' plans to construct a large central car works for the Greater Blackpool Tramways.

In fact, the acquisition of the tramroad turned out to be a less straightforward exercise than the Corporation had expected, due to opposition from the railway companies (L&Y and L&NW) and from Fleetwood UDC, the consequences of which will be discussed in more detail in a later section. Agreement was however reached with all parties during March 1919, and the purchase of the tramroad was finally approved at a meeting of the Town Council on May 6 1919. The Improvement Act received the royal assent on August 15 1919, and the Corporation staff prepared for the amalgamation.

On January 1 1920, John Cameron called at Bispham depôt to collect his mail and then left the tramroad's office for the last time, the richer by £10 000 compensation for loss of office. On the same day, two gangs of Highways Department workmen descended on the tramroad to begin linking up the tracks at the Gynn Inn, where a right-angle junction was to be laid in the street to join

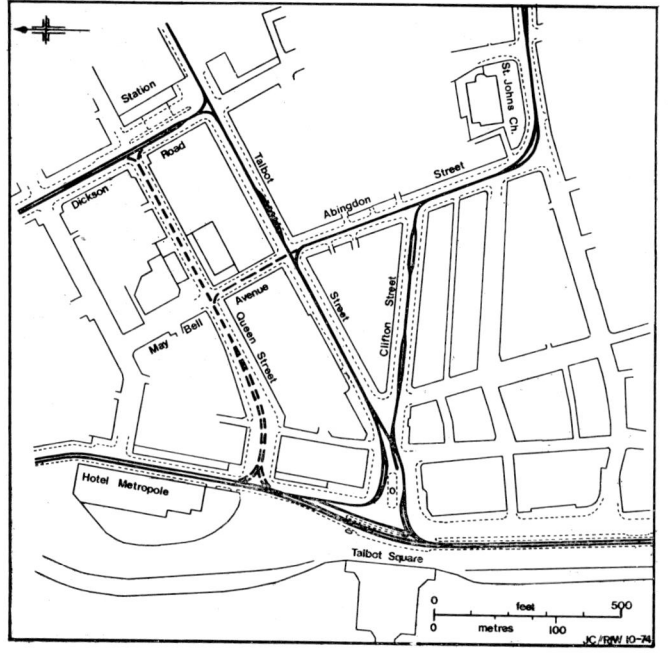

The central Blackpool tramway layout in 1920, after the Corporation had linked the Tramroad with their own line in Talbot Road. The line in Dickson Road, which previously ended in a single-track stub between Springfield Road and Queen Street, was doubled in 1920 and extended to the station entrance, where it became single and then diverged into a triangular junction with the Layton route. The proposed tracks in Queen Street, intended as a terminus for Fleetwood cars, were not built.
(J. C. Cooke, from 'Blackpool by Tram')

the tramroad to the Corporation's North Shore terminus, and at Talbot Road station, where the Company's track was to be extended past the station entrance and round a difficult curve, almost touching the pavement, to meet the single-track-and-loop Layton line in Talbot Road. Another curve gave a connexion towards Layton, so forming a triangular junction.

This double connexion cost altogether some £7 500, which turned out to be quite an extravagance since, as we shall see, the new lines were used only for three months, in 1923, by regular service cars. In fact, the two connexions were the first manifestations of Charles Furness' grand plan for the development of the tramroad. The line was now carrying three times as many passengers as it had done at the turn of the century, though with only seven more cars. Its capacity was limited by the single-track stretches in Dickson Road and particularly by the terminal arrangements which were both crowded and inefficient. When all 41 cars were on the road, cars would be leaving Fleetwood every 1½ minutes.

To improve the capacity of the line, Charles Furness proposed nothing less than the reintroduction of trailers. To speed turn-round, the Fleetwood terminus would be extended in a loop by the Ferry and in Blackpool new lines would be laid in Queen Street and the twin-cars would run into Blackpool via Dickson Road and go out along the Promenade, taking their layover at a terminus in Queen's Square. Until the new line was built the connexion into Talbot Road would have to serve, together with the east-to-north curve put in during 1905 at Talbot Square, and connected since 1911 directly to the northbound Promenade track. The 'Blackpool Times' predicted, a little optimistically, on January 28 1920: *"Before the next season is entered upon, many of the Fleetwood cars (all with trailers) will go along Warbreck Road, Dickson Road and via Talbot Road through the Square and round to the Gynn"*.

Charles Furness himself was more guarded when he explained the reasons for his proposal:

"The acquisition of the undertaking carries with it great responsibilities and it would not be reasonable to expect any great financial benefits in the immediate future. In fact before any appreciable increased traffic can be dealt with, it will be necessary to improve the termini arrangements both in Blackpool and Fleetwood so as to enable trailer cars to be put on service. When this has been brought about it will compensate largely for the higher working expenses brought about by municipal ownership as the working conditions of the employees have been considerably improved since the Corporation acquired the system".

The most significant change in working methods was the closing of the two Fleetwood depôts as running sheds, all cars now running from Bispham depôt. Previously, the last two cars of the day had been housed overnight at Bold Street depôt and others at Copse Road. Of the ten Fleetwood drivers, seven accepted other jobs at Bispham depôt, without reduction in pay and with the promise of driving in summer.

To the travelling public, or those who noticed such things, the first overt sign of the change of ownership was the appearance of Box cars bearing numbers in the range 101-115. The Corporation seems prudently to have used up the stock of the large company numerals at Bispham depôt; a photograph exists of a Box car with the number 106 occupying a large proportion of the dash panel.

The 41 Fleetwood cars were allocated Blackpool Corporation numbers 101 to 141, leaving two spaces after the last Blackpool car, ex-London United No 98. Logically, one would have expected the Corporation to have added 100 to the old numbers, for the sake of simplicity, but instead a rather half-hearted attempt seems to have been made to categorise the Fleetwood cars. Cars 101-105 were eight-window Box cars, 106-115 were the six window cars, 116-125 were the cars with roller shutters ("semi-open" was the official Blackpool description) and 126-141 were open cross-bench cars, but here the system became rather ragged, for there was no attempt to bring together the two almost identical series of open cars 1-10 and 25-27. The renumbering can be briefly summarised in the following table.

Tramroad car renumbering

New no	Old no	Type	Date
101-105	20-24	Box	1899
106-111	14-19	Box	1898
112-115	38-41	Box	1914
116-122	28-34	Yankee	1899
123-125	35-37	Vanguard	1910
126-135	1-10	Old Open	1898
136-138	11-13	ex-Trailer	1898
139-141	25-27	Old Open	1899

In point of fact there is no firm evidence to prove that individual cars were renumbered in sequence within their classes. For the sake of simplicity we will assume that to be the case, but confirmation of the original numbers would be welcomed. The only proven case is that of Box 40 (Blackpool 114, later Engineering car 5), from which the latter-day green paint was carefully removed at Rigby Road in 1960, layer by layer, in order to confirm the original Tramroad livery of ivory, white and teak, to be used in the restoration of the car for Blackpool tramways' 75th anniversary. During this process, the Tramroad number (40) was uncovered.

At the beginning of March 1920 the first Fleetwood Box appeared on the road in the red-and-white Corporation livery. Structurally, the only difference was the fitting of an orthodox electric headlight in place of the old American oil lamp, and the consequent use of the new smaller numerals which could fit over the headlight. To the passenger, though, the most striking change was the disappearance of the prominent roofboard advertisements which had been a feature of the Tramroad cars since 1900. The Tramways Committee at that time was indulging in one of those periods of self-righteousness in regard to advertisements, which most municipal tramways adopted when they could afford it. On March 31 1919, the last advertisement had been removed from the Blackpool cars—a loss of revenue of £700 per annum, about which the Finance Committee was less than pleased. Unfortunately, the contracts for some of the Fleetwood cars had to be honoured until they expired, and for some time municipal pride had to endure the sight of Box car 115 bearing the Corporation livery beneath a prominent advertisement for Iron Jelloids.

Besides the removal of the advertisements, the Corporation take-over was intended to furnish more tangible advantages to the six million passengers which the line now carried each year. In particular Mr Furness announced the introduction of a 10-minute service from April 1 1920 in place of the time-honoured 15-minute basic service which had run as long as anybody could remember.

Achieving a 10-minute service was by no means as easy as it may have sounded. Nine cars would be needed, with another five for the intermediate Cleveleys turnbacks. The Tramroad could only muster a total of 15 saloons, 101-115, and the use of open cars was not always well received, as this letter to the 'Gazette & Herald' from "A Lancashire Woman and a Ratepayer" reveals:

"Open cars were put on the line although the weather was bitterly cold, the rain, hail and wind blowing in making a car ride one long shiver. Elderly persons who had paid their fares were obliged to stand in the cars, as the seats were too wet to sit on".

The ten-minute service was one of the suggestions of the quaintly-named Blackpool & Fleetwood Urgency Sub-Committee which had been set up in 1918 to consider the integration of the Fleetwood route. Their proposal for the Queen Street line had apparently not been supported by Charles Furness, and the Sub-Committee's answer to the shortage of saloons was also at odds with the Manager's intention of buying six new

The only known photograph of a Fleetwood car (No 115) in Corporation livery but still with advertisements on the roofboards, to fulfil unexpired contracts made by the company. The car is crossing the curve put in in 1920 at the Gynn to link Corporation and ex-company tracks. (F. D. Deane

Blackpool "Glasshouse" car 119 at the Gynn in 1920 or 1921, showing how the Corporation rebuilt these cars to 14-window saloons. As shown here the car is on its original Brill bogies, and lacks destination boxes. Compare this view with that of the unrebuilt car on page 26.
(F. D. Deane)

cars. The Sub-Committee's solution was to rebuild some of the open cars into saloons. At first four such rebuilds were recommended, but in February 1920 this was increased to six.

The cars chosen for rebuilding belonged to the "Yankee" class, 116-122, built as Tramroad cars 28-34 in 1899. The work was almost certainly carried out at Bispham, since the new central works at Rigby Road was not yet built and Blundell Street depôt, where the Corporation's maintenance was done, had more than enough work restoring the weary Blackpool fleet to something like pre-war condition. An element of doubt surrounds car 117, which was turned out with red fleur-de-lys quarter-lights of the standard Blackpool type, whilst the other rebuilds had plain glass. Detailed features of the rebuilding suggest that this car might have been converted at Blundell Street as the prototype, though it is said that Fleetwood cars were not at that time capable of running to Blundell Street, presumably because of differences in tyre profiles or the curvature of the tracks in Princess Street.

The conversions produced, as might be expected, an odd-looking vehicle. From the ends the "new" cars presented an unusual but rather attractive aspect with a steeply arched roof culminating in a very distinctive windscreen with two tall and narrow drop windows. From a side view, however, the newly-enclosed cars revealed their origins only too clearly, there being no fewer than 14 windows on each side of the car, these of course representing the original spacing of the pillars on the open sides. The saloon itself extended over only 12 of these windows, the outer ones forming part of the

spacious driver's platforms. This abundance of windows gave the rebuilt cars the unofficial title of "Glass-houses".

Any of the Fleetwood passengers who hoped that the municipal take-over would lead to an increase in comfort as well as frequency were disappointed. The Corporation, of course, was no greater believer in passenger comfort than the Company had been, and the "Glasshouses" had the traditional wooden transverse seats for 48 passengers, seven less than the cars had originally seated. Under the floor, little was changed. The Brill 27D bogies with their American Walker motors were still positioned right at the ends of the car, and this meant that the entrances had to be set at the corner of the body, just as on the other saloons. The original company Box cars of 1898 inherited this feature along with their steam-trailer body construction, but by 1920 it was a complete anachronism. Not only was the entrance high and narrow but, to enable the long 27D bogies to swivel, the bottom step had to be inordinately high off the ground, and the "Glasshouses" soon gained a reputation for being difficult and dangerous to get on and off; lady passengers were sometimes reduced to kneeling on the step before heaving themselves aboard.

Just how many cars were eventually rebuilt is one of those intriguing mysteries which spice the history of Blackpool's tramways between the wars. Photographs exist of cars 116, 117, 119, 120 and 121 as "Glasshouses", but research and discussion over many years has failed to establish for certain whether the sixth conversion was ever carried out. We do know that car 122 was not rebuilt, since it featured in an experiment in 1924 as

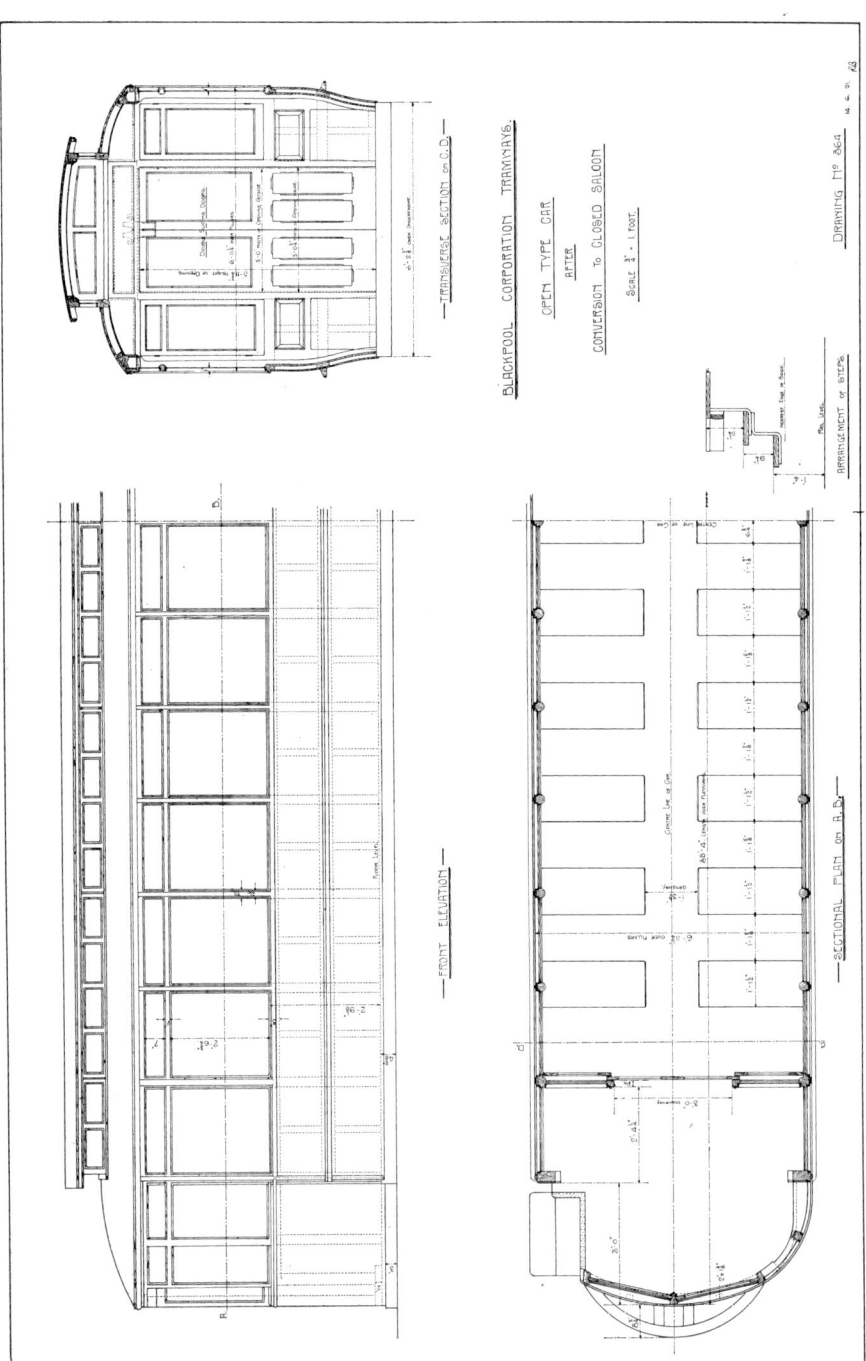

A Blackpool Corporation drawing of 1921 showing the layout of those ex-Tramroad cars in the Corporation's 116-122 series which were rebuilt as enclosed saloons, known unofficially as Glasshouses. Compare this with the drawing on page 25.

an open car. The mystery car amongst the seven "Yankees" is car 118; no photograph has yet been found to prove whether 118 became a "Glasshouse" or not. Corporation records (or at least the handful that have survived the move to Rigby Road, the Town Hall fire, and the wartime paper salvage drives) refer to car 118 in the same light as the other Glasshouses—"rebuilt from shuttered-side car" —but these records are not notably reliable in such details. To illustrate the scepticism with which official records must be regarded, the Tramway accounts for 1920/1 include expenditure of £2 232 for "conversion of eight open cars on the Fleetwood route to closed saloons" and the Tramways Committee minutes of May 30 1921 record an application to the Board of Trade for loan sanction for these eight conversions. Those that were done were carried out between mid-1920 and mid-1921.

The concensus of opinion seems to be that 118 was not rebuilt, and this is borne out by the Tramways Department's summary of rolling stock at March 31 1924, which shows a total of 20 closed saloons. These were presumably cars 101-115 plus the five "Glasshouses": 116, 117, 119, 120 and 121.

Part 6: Towards integration

IT is necessary at this stage to devote some pages to the Corporation's plans to integrate the Tramroad with its existing tramways after the take-over of January 1920. As soon as the Highways Department had finished linking the Tramroad tracks to the Corporation system at Talbot Road and the Gynn in March 1920, the stage was set for the introduction of the radical changes with which Charles Furness was intending to expand the capacity of the Fleetwood line as an integral part of the Greater Blackpool tramways. These would extend for 18 miles from the Ribble to the Wyre, once the Blackpool, St Annes and Lytham company was taken over, which was expected at some time in 1921.

The 1920 Improvement Bill gave the Corporation powers to construct the loop line at Fleetwood Ferry which would be essential before the introduction of the new trailers which Charles Furness had forecast earlier in the year. Powers were also obtained for the proposed Blackpool terminal loop through Queen Square, but the Bill in its final form no longer contained an earlier proposal for a turning circle to be built on the east side of the tracks at Uncle Tom's Cabin. Its deletion from the Bill may be one reason why the twin-car proposal did not materialise.

This proposed turning circle at the Cabin was presumably intended to serve as an intermediate turning point for short-working cars, and as an interchange point with the Promenade and Squires Gate routes. The Corporation, when the take-over was announced in 1918, had suddenly begun to acknowledge the existence of the Tramroad and advertise the merits of taking the Promenade car to the Gynn and catching a Fleetwood excursion from there. In view of the awkward single-track arrangement in Dickson Road, there were obvious advantages in running as many specials as possible from the Gynn, and the turning circle at Cabin would have served the same function when the Corporation cars were extended up the hill. Unfortunately the proposed layout meant crossing Queen's Drive twice, and this is probably why the scheme was abandoned.

The Dickson Road single track had not prevented the Tramroad Company from operating an intensive winter service requiring 12 cars, five on the 15-minute Fleetwood service and the remainder on short workings to the Gynn, Bispham or Cleveleys. The Corporation, as we have seen, introduced a basic 10-minute headway to Fleetwood from April 1 1920, the day before Good Friday. In company days, the Easter holidays would have been a stern test of the new service, since the generating station at Bispham was severely stretched when a large number of cars was out on the line.

This deficiency was most apparent at the Fleetwood end of the line. Because of the length of the feeders from Bispham, which, of course, was not centrally situated, the voltage on the line between Rossall and Fleetwood sometimes fell as low as 320, and at busy times cars were reduced to a crawl. The feeders were also of limited capacity, and there had been

A rare view of Marton Box works car 2 on the Tramroad sleeper track early in 1920, assisting in the laying of the new feeder cable from Uncle Tom's Cabin to Rossall. (Blackpool Corporation

trouble with stray return currents. In 1917 the Postmaster-General sued the company for £16:1:8 for damage caused to a post office cable through electrolysis, but the company had won the case by proving that its line had been built in conformity with Board of Trade regulations.

Charles Furness was also Borough Electrical Engineer, and the generating station at Bispham therefore came within his purview. Not surprisingly, he intended to close the station and replace its obsolete plant by new equipment at the Corporation's West Caroline Street generating station. Work began in 1920 on laying a new feeder cable from Uncle Tom's Cabin to Rossall, in order to supply the whole of the Tramroad from West Caroline Street, but in the meantime a temporary connexion was arranged to the Fleetwood Corporation's supply. This came into effect on Good Friday, April 2, and had a noticeable effect on the speed of the trams, particularly on Easter Monday when no fewer than 40 cars were on the road.

What, meanwhile, was happening to the "grand plan"? How was work progressing on the new terminus in Queen's Square, the loop at Fleetwood Ferry, the new trailers, or even the six Pullman cars? Briefly, it was not. The whole great scheme of 1920 for a new era of municipal development on the Tramroad never got off the ground and, to understand why, we need to step back a little and take a broader view of the Corporation's tramway system.

By an unfortunate mischance, the take-over of the Fleetwood Tramroad coincided with one of the most difficult periods in the whole history of the Corporation tramways. In common with most other British tramway systems, Blackpool ended the war with an immense backlog of maintenance work. Almost every yard of track in the town was due for relaying, and it was only by good fortune that the decision to spend £250 000 on renewing the track was taken a year or two before the introduction of motor buses in the town gave birth to the anti-tram lobby, which was becoming quite influential by 1925. By that time, most of the money had been spent and Blackpool had committed itself to trams for the next 15 years.

The weary state of the track and rolling stock happened to coincide with a post-war boom in passengers which at times in the season reduced the town system to chaos. In 1919 the fleet comprised a mere 84 trams, which included 24 toastracks, leaving the main burden to be borne by only 60 cars, of which 47 were around 20 years old, four nearly 25 years old, and two almost 35 years old. Perhaps the most serious of all the problems, though, was the severe wartime inflation which meant that a top grade driver, who in 1914 had earned 30 shillings for a 60-hour week, was now being paid 70s 6d for 48 hours. The cost of materials, likewise, had increased dramatically since 1914 — rails by 233%, timber by 400%, tickets by 500%.

During the last years of the war, the increase in traffic had helped to disguise the financial problems of the tramway system; it was this continued increase in passengers, too, which eventually helped the undertaking to overcome these problems and repay the massive loan charges which might have crippled a less expansive tramway system. But, for a short period around 1920, the combined effects of the factors outlined above were brought home to the Town Council with considerable force. Compare, as did the Council, the figures for the last full financial year before, and the first year after, the Fleetwood takeover; these are in the table below.

	Year to March 31	
	1919	1921
	£	£
Receipts		
Blackpool	144 535	202 764
Fleetwood	—	81 708
Total	144 535	284 472
Expenses		
Traffic	39 117	105 677
General	18 843	36 172
Maintenance	19 780	57 633
Power	15 899	40 667
Interest	20 844	44 179
Total	114 483	284 328
Net profit	30 052	144

Not surprisingly, these results brought forth a great storm of criticism from councillors who had grown accustomed to at least £10 000 rate relief from the tramways each year. Much incredulity was expressed when Charles Furness reported that in 1920-1 the Fleetwood route had actually made a loss and *"might be regarded by some as poor speculation"*. Ascribing profits and losses to individual routes depends on the method of apportioning overheads, but since the Fleetwood route was still virtually self-contained, the loss could have been genuine. It does seem that the tramroad was missing the intense personal interest which John Cameron had taken in its every detail.

The plan for the Greater Blackpool Tramways received another blow when, on October 29 1920, St Annes Council bought out the Blackpool St Annes & Lytham Tramway Company for £145 000; this proved a bargain only to the company's shareholders, who received their first dividend for 20 years. The blue trams were never a financial success, either before or after the Council takeover, having been burdened with a street tramway system where a Fleetwood-style interurban would have been more suitable.

It was hardly surprising, then, that the great plans for the tramroad were put back on the shelf. The financial results, and a political storm slowly gathering round Charles Furness's head together with the disruption which the vast track renewal programme would entail — all these problems were climaxed by the miners' strike in 1921. Apart from ruining the department's Whitsuntide traffic figures, at a cost of some £11 000, the strike threatened to bring the whole tramway system to a standstill for lack of coal at the power station. Part of Bispham power station was converted to burn oil, but this was not practicable at West Caroline Street, and stocks ran so low that all Sunday trams had to be withdrawn and motor *chars-à-bano* run to the basic tram timetable.

The coal shortage gave the Fleetwood route a chance to redeem its slightly

Fleetwood box car 108 in Blackpool Corporation red and white livery at Gynn Square, photographed by C. T. Humpidge in 1926. The car's fleet number was repeated on the former advertising roofboards.
(C. T. Humpidge)

Above: The first Tramroad car to be withdrawn from passenger service was 139, which became a works car in 1924. It is seen here in 1925 removing one of the boilers from the Tramroad company's former generating station at Bispham depôt, which had been closed by the Corporation.
(Blackpool Corporation

Below: "Glasshouse" car 117 waiting to turn out of the Red Bank Road depôt line at Bispham. This car differed from the rest of the class in having fleur-de-lys quarter lights and no rainstrip.
(Dr H. A. Whitcombe, courtesy Science Museum)

tarnished reputation. By some devious means the Corporation had contrived to beat the strike by arranging a consignment of Belgian coal which arrived by ship at Fleetwood.

Since the railway unions refused to deliver the coal, the Corporation hit on the idea of smuggling it into Blackpool over the tramroad, using a train of permanent-way wagons which ran to and fro over the new Gynn link. The coal was presumably taken by cart to Copse Road depôt at Fleetwood, and similarly transhipped from Blundell Street to the nearby power station. In Blackpool, the train was normally hauled by rebuilt Marton Box 31 (the present works car 754), which would take over from a Fleetwood car at the Gynn. The Blackpool car was unlikely to have ventured all the way to Fleetwood, since the difference in tyre profiles would have made the chances of derailment too high, particularly on the sharp curve which then existed by Rossall School.

Five years were to pass before the Tramways Department achieved any significant improvements in the working of the Fleetwood route, and we shall see in the next part how these changes were made possible by the track-laying activities of the Borough Surveyor between 1923 and 1926. The only notable event on the operating side was instigated from outside the Department in May 1924, when a very interesting experiment was carried out by English Electric at Bispham depôt, continuing the tradition of co-operation between the Tramroad and Preston works. Bispham was still operating as a separate entity from the main works at Rigby Road, under the control of Angus Cameron, the former General Manager's brother, who had been the company's engineer and had stayed on after the takeover. English Electric had developed a new type of lightweight camshaft controller for use in multiple-unit operation and had received an order from the British Columbia Electric Railway of

Vancouver. To test the equipment, English Electric took over two of the former "Yankee" cars, No 121, an enclosed "Glasshouse", and No 122, still in original condition, and ran them in multiple-unit. The control equipment was mounted under the centre of each car, and tested under "live" conditions. The two cars quite probably ran in passenger service when operating singly, but never did so in multiple-unit; this would not have been permissible without Ministry of Transport authority.

If English Electric was hoping to interest Blackpool in its new controllers, it was disappointed, though not even the most optimistic manufacturer could have envisaged the Blackpool tramways of the mid-twenties as a customer for such advanced equipment; tramcar development on the Corporation system had virtually stood still since 1911. In fairness, it should be mentioned that Blackpool had achieved a lower power consumption than any other major British municipal tramway—less than 1.5 kWh/car-mile—and would naturally tend to standardise on the simple and reliable equipment that made this possible. But the experiment seems to have jogged the Corporation's memory about the twin-car proposals, for there followed a little flurry of activity which seemed as if it might presage a revived interest in trailer operation.

Work began at the end of 1924 on the turning circle at Fleetwood Ferry, thus isolating the old company depôt at Bold Street which the Corporation had not used since early 1920. Construction began only just in time, since the powers under the 1920 Improvement Act expired on August 4 1925. It was too late to begin work on the Queen Street line in Blackpool, which was included in the same Act, but the trailer proposals must still have had some support, for the Queen Street link was included in the new 1925 Improvement Act, thereby extending the powers to August 1930.

Since 1920-21 when the Glasshouses were converted, the 41 Fleetwood cars had remained more or less unchanged. In 1924 the first withdrawal took place, when crossbench car 139 was removed

Blackpool Corporation enclosed car 121 and open car 122 outside Bispham depôt in May 1924, during trials with English Electric multiple-unit equipment built for export. (GEC Traction

from passenger service and became a works car at Bispham, with the running boards removed from its bogies to enable it to negotiate the sharper curves of the Blackpool town system, though this does not seem to have happened often. When the Lancashire boilers were taken out of Bispham generating station in May 1925, they were towed by car 139, but their journey through Blackpool to Rigby Road yard, for shipment by rail to Burnley, was made behind ex-Marton Box works car 2.

Bispham power station had closed down during the previous winter, and the old boiler house was adapted to store fittings for the illuminations, which were introduced in 1925. The most popular feature of the new "lights" was the illuminated gondola car, built on the frame of Marton "Box" car 28. The gondola was not permitted to travel over the tramroad north of the Cabin, since its tyres were not suitable for running on Vignoles rail, but an exception was made at the end of the lights when the car was driven up to Fleetwood to be stored for the winter in Copse Road depôt. This became a regular arrangement for the gondola and later the lifeboat, and lasted until more depôt space became available in Blackpool, but the trip was so fraught with peril for a four-wheel tram that it was always made with an engineering car following and a tower wagon alongside on the road.

These events of 1924-25 have taken us a little beyond the main story, and in the next section we shall return to 1922 and trace the effect on the Tramroad of the widespread track renewal and relocation carried out in 1923 and 1924 on both the routes by which Tramroad cars could make their entry into Blackpool.

Part 7: Diversions and relaying

ON December 9 1922, passengers who boarded the Fleetwood cars at Talbot Road station were surprised to find that the guard had omitted to change the seats round at the terminus. They were even more surprised when the tram set off in the wrong direction, turned right at the triangular junction, and then picked its way carefully down Talbot Road before coming to a halt at the side of the road outside the Whittle Springs bar. There followed a pause of a minute or so whilst one of the grotesque Marton Box cars ground its way past on the single track towards Layton Cemetery. Then the Fleetwood Box swung back into the middle of the road and rolled slowly down into Talbot Square.

The sight of a Fleetwood single-decker outside the Town Hall caused even the most casual observer to take a second glance before the Box car moved off over the rarely-used curve which led from the Layton terminus to the northbound Promenade track by the Metropole Hotel. From there the route lay along the street and up through Claremont Park to the Gynn, where the car continued past the North Shore terminus and over the sharp left hand curve in Gynn Square to become once more a common-or-garden Fleetwood tram.

The reason for these unusual manoeuvres was the beginning, at last, of the widening of Dickson and Warbreck Roads and the doubling of the track. To reduce tram traffic whilst the work was in progress, the outward Fleetwood cars were diverted to the Promenade, leaving only a two-car shuttle running each way between Talbot Road and the Gynn. After two weeks, on December 21 1922, this shuttle, too, was withdrawn and the entire service between Blackpool terminus and the Gynn was run as a circular.

The practicalities of running down Talbot Road must have been nerve-wracking for the inspector at the station. The Fleetwood service consisted of seven cars, plus four on Cleveleys turnbacks and another four running to Bispham. This meant despatching a car from Blackpool approximately every three minutes. There was only one loop in Talbot Road, at the Whittle Springs, and when this was inserted the Corporation had agreed not to use it when beer was being delivered. Talbot Road was already inadequate for the Layton service, which one of its drivers once described as "a dizzy run", comprising four cars on a six-minute service and up to four specials, often running in tandem with the service cars to reduce congestion on the single track.

This temporary diversion for the winter of 1922-3, marked the beginning of the Fleetwood route's integration with the rest of the Blackpool system. Curiously, the town tramways themselves had always been fragmented, there being little linking or overlapping between the Layton, Marton or Squires Gate services, whilst the two company routes from Lytham and Fleetwood both crept furtively into town along the back roads to their termini at Central and Talbot Road railway stations. There was little impression of a busy tramway system; rather one of a collection of individual routes.

Suddenly the great track renewal programme changed all that. The Fleetwood cars appeared in Talbot Square for the first time on December 9 1922. Then, on January 22 1923, the relaying of Central Drive brought about the diversion of the blue Lytham St Annes cars straight along Lytham Road and on to the Promenade, to reverse at Talbot Square on the siding outside North Pier. The Fleetwood and Lytham companies had for years been trying to gain access to the Promenade and to link up with each other, and a certain amount of cynicism was expressed at the ease with which this could be accomplished now that both systems were municipalised.

Finally, on February 5 1923, the Marton service from Talbot Square to Central Station was diverted from Central Drive to the Promenade to form another temporary circular route via Lytham Road back to Talbot Square. For the next few weeks the Square was witness to a veritable pageant of trams such as had never been seen in winter before, or indeed since.

The year 1923 marked the beginning of great changes for the tramways in the north of the town, which had seen barely any improvement since they were laid down at the turn of the century. In January, work began on a new cantilevered footpath along Claremont Park, or what is now North Promenade. Once this was completed the tram tracks could be removed from their awkward position at the side of the carriageway and replaced by a new paved reservation on the site of the old footpath. At the north end of the reservation the tracks would join those from Dickson Road (Warbreck Road as it then was) at a new junction in Gynn Square. This would then lead to the old Tramroad paved reservation which would be extended up the hill to Uncle Tom's Cabin.

The summer of 1923 restored some semblance of normality to the Blackpool system, but at the end of the season the tracks were torn up again all over the town and the Fleetwood cars once more figured prominently in the diversions. This time it was the turn of the Warbreck Road track to be doubled, and the Tramways Department, having presumably shuddered at the prospect of running the circular Fleetwood service again, decided to abandon Warbreck Road altogether to the Highways Department and to run a bus service from Talbot Road station to the Gynn, only the third bus route to be operated by the Corporation.

On January 3 1924, the trams were accordingly diverted along the Promenade to reverse in Talbot Square. Although this kept the Fleetwood cars clear of the reconstruction work in Warbreck Road, it meant that they were thrown right into the middle of the upheaval on North Promenade where the northern end of the new reservation was nearing completion. For the first few weeks the Fleetwood trams used the old Gynn junction and the street track down to Talbot Square, but by March the new junction was almost complete and the Fleetwood and North Shore cars were diverted on to the new reservation at the Gynn and travelled as far as Warley Road before rejoining the North Promenade street track by a temporary reverse curve. As work on North Promenade progressed through the summer—much to the residents' disgust—the reservation was extended piecemeal from each end, and these temporary curves gained considerable notoriety, having been laid so crudely that at one time a gang was stationed permanently outside the Fernley Hotel to extricate derailed trams.

The new layout at the Gynn included a third track on the landward side of the reservation, which was meant to serve cars in both directions. Trams from Blackpool could enter the third track by a facing crossover on the bend just south of the square, whilst Fleetwood excursions could run straight into the third track from the north end, having loaded, run wrong-road over the junction to reach the top crossover.

The Gynn junction was completed on April 15 1924 and, next day, the Fleetwood cars returned to the widened Warbreck Road. The temporary bus service had proved so popular, however, that it was amended to run from Talbot Square to Warley Road by another route. Eventually it was given service number 3, and survives to this day, though extended to Marton. On Warbreck Road the new double track had been laid, but an unfortunate dispute over acquisition of property meant that the road widening had not been completed. Between Pleasant Street and Derby Road the trams had to run single-line along the northbound track, an arrangement which was to last for over two years.

The day after the Fleetwood cars left the Promenade, the frontier between the Tramroad and the Corporation system at the Gynn was removed. At 14.01 hrs on April 17 1924, the first Blackpool double-decker operated over the Tramroad on the Cabin—Squires Gate service. The fenced sleeper track between the Cabin and the old Borough boundary had been relaid as a paved reservation in the same style as the new track which was being laid on North Promenade, using bullhead rail with an angle-iron check rail to permit double-deck operation.

Further north, another improvement was under way on the Tramroad. When the line was built in 1897-8, the section between Rossall and Fleetwood Road (later Broadwater) was laid with an acute "dog's leg" for reasons now long forgotten but presumably connected with the purchase of land. The Blackpool and Fleetwood Tramroad Act of 1896 gave the company powers to alter the course of this section, should it interfere with the construction of a new direct road between Cleveleys and Fleetwood. It is a tribute to the far-sightedness of those who drafted the Bill, or an indictment of those who were planning the new road, that the powers were not exercised for almost 30 years.

The new road was opened in 1931, but the line was diverted well in advance. The Corporation were keen to relocate the line, not only to reduce the length of their route by some 300 yards, but also to eliminate dewirements which were a regular occurrence on the sharp bend of the old line, particularly in high winds. On the night of Saturday, May 9 1925, the 23.28 Box car from Fleetwood to Bispham made the last journey along the old southbound track; immediately the car had passed, a gang of men set to work to lay in connexions to the new line. By morning the job was not finished, and the first two cars from Bispham had to be run through to Fleetwood and then operate a shuttle service over the old northbound track from Stanley Road to Rossall. There passengers had to circumnavigate the excavations and board one of the five cars which were running between Rossall and Talbot Road, single-line only as far as Cleveleys. Finally, at 13.40 hrs, the connexions were completed and Box car 111, running the 13.30 from Fleetwood, inaugurated service on the new southbound track. The old northbound track remained in use until Saturday July 4 1925, when another all-night session allowed the new line to come into use with the first car of Sunday morning. The old alignment was abandoned completely, and today its course is barely distinguishable.

Meanwhile, the new loop line at Fleetwood Ferry had been opened on May 30

The new layout completed in April 1924 at Gynn Square, showing de luxe bogie car 66 and the third track. During the winter the Tramroad from this point to Uncle Tom's Cabin was relaid as a paved reservation, ready for the new Squires Gate—Cabin service which commenced on April 17 1924.
(Valentine & Sons

1925, in time for Whitsuntide, and proved a great convenience for passengers travelling to the railway station and the Knott End ferry. The circular tours of the Over Wyre district also benefitted, and the Corporation's share of receipts from its Pilling circular tour increased from £677 in 1924 to £855. This tour comprised a return tram ride from Talbot Road, a crossing on the Knott End ferry and a ride to Pilling on a motor char-à-banc of Fleetwood & Knott End Motors Ltd. It ran from 1923 to 1927.

Construction of the Ferry loop meant that the Fleetwood line now had, theoretically at least, turning loops at each end of the route, but there was no sign of the trailer project being revived. Integration of the Fleetwood line, too, had progressed little beyond the running of town cars to the Cabin; despite the awkward length of single-track running on Dickson Road and the completion of the North Promenade reservation at the end of 1924, the Fleetwood service was still run from Talbot Road station. There was a solitary exception to this rule; from June 13 to September 23 1925, a single car ran to Talbot Square each morning and returned at 09.45 as the "Isle of Man Boat Tram" connecting with the 10.30 steamer from Fleetwood to Douglas.

The Tramways Department's lack of enthusiasm for running the Fleetwood cars on the Promenade was probably due to the state of the track, which had been in very poor condition owing, it is said, to the foundations having been laid on top of the old sloping sea-wall when the Promenade was widened in 1905. The tyre profile of the Tramroad cars was not suitable for efficient running on the old grooved rail with which the Promenade was laid. Since the great track reconstruction programme began, most of the Promenade route had been relaid with sleeper track, a type of construction which the borough surveyor, Francis Wood, strongly favoured. Instead of the old grooved rail with concrete paving, the new track was laid in bullhead rail with angle-iron check rail and paved with pre-cast concrete slabs, and this of course removed any restrictions on the Tramroad cars running through.

The final section of the Promenade route, at North Pier, was due to be relaid in 1926 and, at the same time, the open Tramroad tracks between Cabin and Bispham were to be rebuilt with bullhead and check rail in place of the old Vignoles rail which the company had used. When this was done, Blackpool cars would be able to travel as far north as Bispham, and Fleetwood cars would have the run of the entire Promenade. At last, six years after the Corporation take-over, the integration of the Fleetwood route with the town system would be a reality.

Meanwhile, there was still one major improvement to be carried out at Fleetwood. The tracks in Lord Street and North Albert Street remained much as they had been in 1898, being widely-spaced double track with ornamental centre poles which gave a touch of elegance to an otherwise undistinguished town centre. Fleetwood Council, however, wanted the centre poles removed since they were something of an obstruction to the increasing motor traffic, and was pressing Blackpool to reconstruct the entire track from Ash Street to the Ferry loop.

This section of track had always been subject to an 8-miles/h speed restriction, a limit which the Tramways Department applied to have doubled. Fleetwood Council objected in view of the state of the track, and on February 23 1926 Lt-Col Mount of the Ministry of Transport visited Fleetwood to discuss the proposal. A trial run was made along Lord Street at the suggested speed of 16 miles/h, and this proved hair-raising enough to convince the Inspector that the original limit would have to remain until Blackpool relaid the track.

The work began on January 27 1927, when Blackpool Highways Department workmen started tearing up the tracks near the old Bold Street terminus. The project involved widening the roadway, replacing the centre poles with side poles and span wire, and relaying the track with closer spacing. Fleetwood Council was never too pleased to see Blackpool Corporation digging up its main street, but in this case it gained financially since the cost of the work was borne jointly by Blackpool, Fleetwood and Lancashire County Council, Lord Street qualifying as one of the county's main roads.

At first the Fleetwood cars reversed in North Albert Street, but on March 4 1927 the trams were stopped at Ash Street, the end of the reservation, and a connecting bus service was run from there to Pharos Street by an alternative route. Complete closure of the line enabled the work to be pushed forward and finished just in time, on the day before the Easter holiday began. The importance which Fleetwood placed on the work can be judged from the fact that the Chairman of the Highways Committee completed the job by welding the last pair of rails, and at 10.30 hrs on the morning of April 14 1927, Box car 109 inaugurated the new track, the first car to run to the Ferry for nearly three months.

Part 8: A year to remember

SEASIDE tramways, by their very nature, respond to such wide variations in traffic that their operations seldom remain static for long enough to become monotonous to the enthusiast. To followers of Blackpool tramway affairs no two summer seasons are quite the same, each producing its own pattern of operation and usage of rolling stock. Against this constantly evolving background, however, certain years stand out as being especially memorable in terms of tramway interest. To Blackpool enthusiasts of the postwar generation, the summer of 1960, for instance, saw the tramcar fleet reach the point of maximum interest and variety whilst, in prewar years, the 1934 season had represented a similar watershed in the development of Blackpool's rolling stock.

There was one other year, 1926, which seemed similarly to be crowded with tramway landmarks, although there were few, if any, local enthusiasts to savour it. The dramatic events of 1926 were provided not by rolling stock changes but by the changing pattern of services and by political events, both local and national. 1926 saw the most radical upheaval in the operation of the Promenade and Fleetwood routes since the tramways had been opened between 1885 and 1900.

Passengers on the early-morning commuter specials, which ran on the Tramroad to connect with the Manchester trains from Talbot Road, had the first inkling of unusual events afoot on the morning of April 9. As they approached Bispham the more observant passengers might have noticed that the "turnback" car waiting at the station was not the usual "Box" saloon, but a double-deck Blackpool Standard car, a sight which had never been seen before on the Fleetwood Tramroad. On that one day only, the Talbot Road—Bispham short workings were being operated by double-deckers from Blundell Street, the first time that such cars had ever run in service north of the Cabin. Exactly why

UEC box car 112 passing Fleetwood lighthouse in Pharos Street after the completion of the Ferry loop
(S. L. Smith

this was done we do not know—perhaps as a trial of the track between Cabin and Bispham, which had just been relaid with bullhead and check rail—but the experiment was never repeated and double-deckers remained a great rarity on Dickson Road until 1936.

By an odd chance, though, only three days went by before double-deckers appeared for a second time on Dickson Road, but not this time in service. On April 12 1926, work had begun on the final stage of relaying the Promenade line, involving the short but complex stretch of track between Church Street and Queen's Square. The entire length of track was taken up, including the junctions into Talbot Square, and cars from the south were turned back at Church Street. This left the problem of how to operate the rest of the Promenade route, from Queen's Square to the Cabin. Blundell Street cars could reach North Promenade only by making an enormous detour round the Marton route, whilst Bispham's spare cars were all open-sided and even the five with roller shutters (118 and 122-125) were hardly suitable for early morning and late night services. The problem was solved by using five cars from Marton depôt, probably old top-covered Motherwells of the 42-53 class; each morning these five cars would leave Marton for Talbot Square, reverse there on to the Layton tracks to run up Talbot Road, and then turn left along Dickson Road to join the Promenade route at the Gynn.

The completion of the Talbot Square relaying would open up the entire Promenade route to the Fleetwood cars, but unfortunately, just as the final touches were being put to the new tracks, the entire undertaking was paralysed by the General Strike. The strike came into effect at midnight on May 3-4 1926, and no trams ran on any route until 17.00 on May 13, the longest stoppage in the history of the Blackpool tramways. Services of a sort were maintained by a fleet of motor *chars-à-banc* which operated on all tram routes, despite occasional intimidation from tramwaymen.

As a brief prelude to the introduction of regular Promenade—Fleetwood working, the Tramroad cars were diverted to

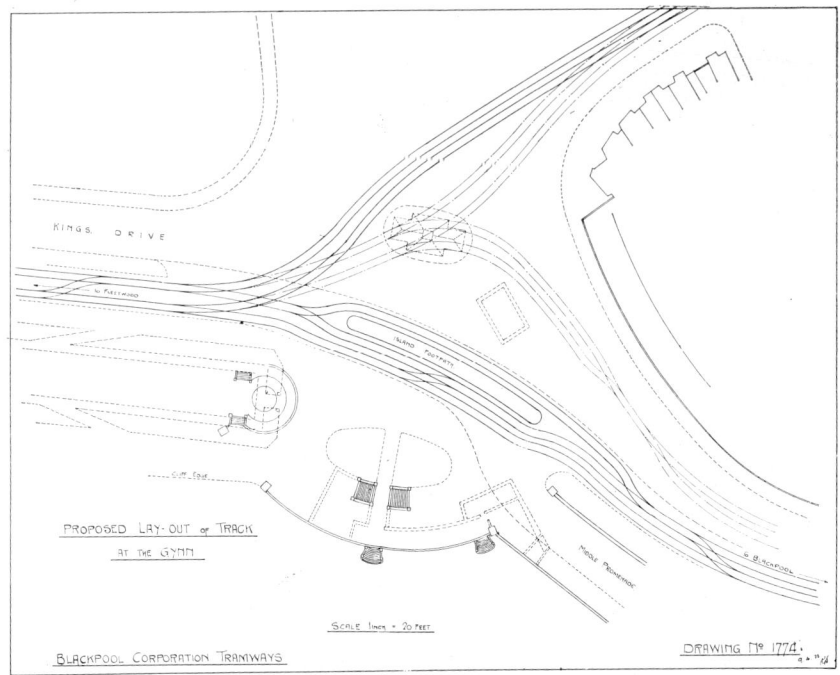

An official Blackpool Corporation drawing of the new 1924 layout at Gynn Square, showing the old and new track arrangement. From July 23 1926, this became the terminus of the blue car service from Lytham. As built, the tracks from the Dickson Road route followed a straighter, more northerly course than that shown.

Talbot Square for the morning of June 20, until at 12.36 hrs the southbound track in Warbreck Road between Derby Road and Pleasant Street was brought into commission, more than two years after it had been laid. The long-delayed widening of this section meant that the entire route between Talbot Road station and Fleetwood was now double track.

The first permanent route alteration of 1926 came on June 25, when the Promenade service was extended from Uncle Tom's Cabin to Bispham, bringing Dreadnoughts, Motherwells, toastracks and London United cars to the Tramroad proper for the first time. Bispham now assumed the rôle of "frontier post" between the town system and the Fleetwood section, a rôle which, to a gradually lessening degree, it has retained ever since.

The Tramways Department wisely did not attempt to introduce the entire new pattern of operations at one fell swoop, preferring a more gradual adjustment of the familiar methods of working. Fleetwood trams were to remain confined to Dickson Road for some months yet, although an exception was made on July 1 when five cars operated special trips from Talbot Square to take visitors on an inspection tour of HMS Empress of India which was berthed at Fleetwood.

The changes on the Promenade had repercussions along the whole 18 miles of the coastal tramway, from Fleetwood to Lytham. Tied in with the alterations in Blackpool was a re-organisation of the "blue car" service between Talbot Square and the Cottage Hospital at Lytham, which came into effect on July 23. On that day the Lytham cars were extended

Above: On June 25 1926, Blackpool Corporation extended the Promenade tram service from Uncle Tom's Cabin to Bispham, over track newly relaid with bullhead and check rail to admit double-deck cars. This 1927 view at Bispham station shows a Dreadnought of the 17-26 class unloading behind one of the ex-Company 1914 Box cars, 112-115.
(TMS

Below: Another Dreadnought photographed in August 1934, passing the Miners' Convalescent Home, between Cabin and Bispham.
(G. L. Gundry

north from Talbot Square, where they had been causing congestion, to the Gynn, thus finally achieving the old companies' aim of linking the Fleetwood and Lytham routes. There was a debit side to this reorganisation, for on the previous night the blue cars had run for the final time on the 0.8-mile of track between Lytham Square and the Cottage Hospital. This short line, which might have become part of the estuarial tramway to Southport described in *Modern Tramway* for July 1969, was the last new route (at that time) to have been opened in the Fylde, and now became the first to be closed.

The Fleetwood cars at last managed to penetrate south of Talbot Square from August 22 1926, when a new "excursion" service began from Manchester Square to Fleetwood. The service loaded at the third track in the roadway, which had previously been used by Lytham short-workings, and it was operated by nine crossbench cars. The excursion service was quite heavily promoted by the Tramways Department, posters at each tram shelter announcing "Special Through Cars to Fleetwood run each Morning and Afternoon from Manchester Square via Promenade. Fare 9d." This was 1d dearer than the fare which applied from Talbot Road Station. Return tickets at one shilling were also available between Talbot Road and Fleetwood, except during the month of August.

For 1926 the Tramways Department had produced an enlarged scheme of Illuminations stretching from the Gynn to South Shore, and on the opening night, September 25, a special excursion service was operated, at a fare of 10d, all the way from Fleetwood to the Pleasure Beach. The layout at the Pleasure Beach had been revised during the previous winter, in readiness for the extension of the Promenade route to Clifton Drive. The new layout, which came into operation on April 1 1926, provided much more storage space than the previous four-track dead-end, which would have been hard pressed to accommodate the Fleetwood cars.

The Fleetwood—Pleasure Beach service lasted for only three days before the 1926 Illuminations were closed down by the Ministry of Mines, who threatened to commandeer the generating station unless Blackpool stopped flouting the emergency restrictions on display lighting brought about by the Coal Strike. But the Lights shone, as it happened, for one more day, to mark the opening of the new South Promenade by Lord Derby on October 2. At 11.40 hrs on that day, Blackpool toastrack No 82 inaugurated the extended tramway from the Pleasure Beach to Clifton Drive, but the new line was not used regularly until the following summer.

Running the Fleetwood cars along the Promenade brought one minor operational problem—the side destination screens of the saloons were limited to the Dickson Road route, and the open cars had no route indicators at all. To overcome this, the Fleetwood cars were fitted with "route letter" boxes, which indicated—just—what service the car was running; northbound, "F" for Fleetwood and "C" for Cleveleys; southbound, "B" for Blackpool (Talbot Road) and "P" for Promenade. These singularly useless letters had to be augmented by small metal plates hung on the dash, in order to satisfy an agreement signed with the Pleasure Beach Company on February 23 1917, when the transfer of land for the new South Promenade was negotiated. Section 16 of this Agreement specified that "a destination indicator bearing the words 'Pleasure Beach' shall be exhibited on the outside of all tramcars completing their southerly journey at the present tramways terminus at South Shore for a period of 15 years from the date when the trams shall commence to run on the new promenade".

During 1926 another of the Fleetwood cars was withdrawn, and this casualty, Box car 101, is something of a mystery. The Corporation were still short of rolling stock for the Tramroad, particularly saloons, and there is no indication of why 101 was discarded; certainly no serious accidents were reported at this time. Nor is it clear what became of 101. The rolling stock totals at March 31 1928 include a "bogie freight car" which was not listed two years previously, and it is tempting to speculate that 101 was converted into a freight car for use on the goods and mineral service which was due to start in 1927. Against this, though, is the fact that the rolling stock returns used the term "freight car" to cover a multitude of things, including works cars and permanent way wagons.

The expansive events of 1926 took place against a background of political crisis. Whilst not wishing to delve into tedious details, some knowledge of local politics is essential for an understanding of the course of tramway development in Blackpool during the 1920's.

We have already seen how, in 1920, the decision was taken to relay all the track in Blackpool during the next three or four years, thereby pre-empting any major controversy over the retention of the trams before the emergence of the pro-bus lobby in the Council. Inevitably, the anti-tram movement began to gather force, encouraged by the relative popularity of the Corporation's new bus service and by the reports of abandonments elsewhere in the transport press. The virulence of their arguments was heightened, rather than lessened, by their relative impotence in the face of the massive investment which had just been made in the tramway system.

The leader of the bus faction, Councillor Tatham, conducted what amounted to a personal campaign against Charles Furness, "that Prince of Bureaucrats" as he described the manager, or on another occasion "that autocratic ruler of the destinies of our local tram service". Poor Charles Furness, who by common consent seems to have been a "gentleman of the old school" was forced to endure indignity after indignity in the Council Chamber; at one Tramways Committee meeting in 1924, Councillor Tatham was reported as saying that he would not listen to "this Juggernaut; he is here to be instructed and not to give instruction". The growing criticism in the Town Council was no doubt the reason for the more or less misleading information which was sometimes presented to the Committee, in particular the classic rebuilding fiction which charged brand-new Standard cars to the revenue account, instead of trying to obtain official sanction for capital expenditure, with the risk that it might have been turned down.

The opposition, wisely enough, concentrated their efforts on removing the transport side of the undertaking from Charles Furness' control. His post as Borough Electrical Engineer and Tramways Manager—"the phrase has a rather Mikadian touch" said Councillor Tatham—also included responsibility for the Illuminations and other special events. This sort of joint control of electricity and transport had been normal practice in earlier days when the two were more closely related, but since the war the introduction of motor buses and the growing complexity of the electrical industry had encouraged a trend towards separate management.

The climax of this rather one-sided battle of personalities arrived on July 7 1926, when the General Purposes Committee, which was in fact the entire Council, recommended by 25 votes to 22 the separation of the departments and the appointment of "a modern transport specialist to remodel the existing transport system". A further meeting was held on July 15 to discuss this thinly-veiled insult to the Manager, and it was here that the bus lobby, when they appeared to be at the very point of success, made a dreadful error of judgment which perhaps in a single moment sealed the future of the Blackpool tramway system. At this second meeting the Mayor had arranged, as a belated act of courtesy, for Charles Furness to give his views on the matter, there having been some criticism that he was not invited to the original meeting. As soon as the Manager was called to address the Committee, fourteen members of the opposing faction stood up and walked out of the Council Chamber.

Even by the none-too-gentlemanly standards of Blackpool politics, this was an act of such appalling rudeness that the main issue was soon totally overshadowed. Charles Furness handed in his resignation in protest at the discourtesy extended to him as the Council's professional adviser. A grudging vote of 22 to 18 the following day, asking the Manager to reconsider his decision, was transformed by a wave of Press and public support into a 31 to 5 vote on July 28 in favour of retaining joint control and expressing total confidence in Mr Furness' management.

So it was that the Blackpool tramways continued for another 6½ years under the aegis of one of the staunchest supporters of tramcars. From 1926 until Mr Furness left the Transport Department in 1932, public criticism of the tramways virtually ceased, a welcome change from the almost constant bickering of the 1924-26 period. When he died in October 1943, *Modern Tramway* headed his obituary "The man who saved Blackpool's trams".

At this distance in time, it is only fair to say that the advocates of separate control had a strong case. Both tramway and electricity undertakings were growing at an enormous rate, not to mention the new Illuminations, and on the tramway side the Department seemed to be struggling just to maintain the status quo. There had been no significant development in the tramcar fleet for 15 years, and the twelve new cars which had just been ordered were virtual replicas of the De Luxe cars and toastracks of 1911.

We shall see in a later part how the vote of confidence was followed by a

The through service from Fleetwood to the Promenade commenced on August 22 1926, initially to Manchester Square but extended on September 25-28 to the Pleasure Beach. It became a regular service in the following season, worked exclusively by ex-Tramroad Company cars. These three photographs show, **above**, "Vanguard" cross-bench car 123 at Fleetwood Ferry terminus, with a 106-111 class car behind: **centre**, "Glasshouse" car 121 at Pleasure Beach, about to return to Fleetwood; **below**, "New Box" car 113 at South Pier. The route letter boxes displayed "B" for Blackpool (Talbot Road), "C" for Cleveleys, "F" for Fleetwood and "P" for Promenade, the Promenade cars also carrying a metal plate reading "Pleasure Beach and Fleetwood". These three photographs were taken in 1931.
(M. J. O'Connor)

burst of activity to modernise the Fleetwood rolling stock, as Charles Furness' management began to regain some of the momentum of the early days after the take-over in 1920. The Council meeting of July 15 1926 proved to be a turning-point in the fortunes of the Blackpool tramways; it does not seem an exaggeration to suggest that had the anti-Furness faction not overplayed their hand on that day, control of the tramways would have passed to a "modern transport specialist", and by the late 1930's Blackpool's tramways would probably have ceased to exist. And this history would have ended a good deal sooner than it is going to do!

Part 9: The coal trains

AT this point in our story we must go back some nine years to July 17 1918 when Alderman Lindsay Parkinson, Mayor and later Member of Parliament for Blackpool, announced that he had secured sufficient share options to guarantee a controlling interest in the Fleetwood Tramroad Company. The transformation of these options into an official take-over by the Corporation turned out to be a less straightforward exercise than had been expected, and the debate which followed was to have a lasting effect on the form and operation of the Tramroad.

The take-over was to be authorised by the Blackpool Improvement Bill of 1919, and the drafting of this Bill was well under way when the first shot of the unexpected battle was fired. The Lancashire & Yorkshire and London & North Western Railway companies (who jointly operated the Preston & Wyre railways) had been prospective purchasers of the Tramroad themselves, their approaches having been thwarted by Lindsay Parkinson's swift action in gaining personal control of the company. The railway companies responded by announcing on November 22 1918 details of their own Bill for a branch railway to run from Thornton to a station just east of Victoria Square at Cleveleys.

It is hard to believe that the railways were in earnest with this proposal *per se*, since the potential traffic would be small, and the scheme seems more political than practical. It certainly worried the Corporation, which was concerned that the railways might demand a junction with the Tramroad and running powers over the line to Fleetwood. At that time, it must be remembered, the railways had a near monopoly of transport in the area, and widespread interests in Fleetwood.

Opposition from another quarter was declared on January 17 1919 when Fleetwood Urban District Council announced that it would oppose the Blackpool Corporation Bill. Fleetwood was furious that it had not been invited to participate in the ownership of the Tramroad, nearly half of which lay in its territory. The Council had understood from Lindsay Parkinson that the line was available for all the local authorities to purchase, and was hoping that the Tramroad would be run by a Joint Committee on the lines of the Fylde Water Board. The Mayor denied having given any such undertaking, and there followed some acrimonious correspondence between Lindsay Parkinson and the Fleetwood Chairman, and some fairly wild talk in the Fleetwood council chamber about plans to purchase their section of the Tramroad and construct a new loop line along the Promenade to Rossall. The street tramway in Fleetwood was operated under legislation which would permit Corporation purchase in 1928, but the tramroad from Ash Street to the boundary at Rossall was held by the Company in perpetuity.

Negotiations with Fleetwood were protracted, and agreement reached only on the morning of March 26 1919, when the case was about to be heard in London. Fleetwood was given the option of purchasing the entire line within the borough after 21 years. If Fleetwood purchased the line, Blackpool had the right to a further 21 years' lease. If Fleetwood did not purchase the line, as turned out to be the case, the powers would lapse. The Corporation undertook that the Fleetwood service would run to the same frequency as the short-working Cleveleys cars and agreed to other minor clauses, including the provision of special workmen's fares in Fleetwood.

Sitting very pretty in the middle of all this was the Thornton Urban District Council, through whose territory ran the strategic mile in the middle of the Tramroad. Blackpool had almost concluded an agreement to incorporate Thornton and its satellite Cleveleys into the

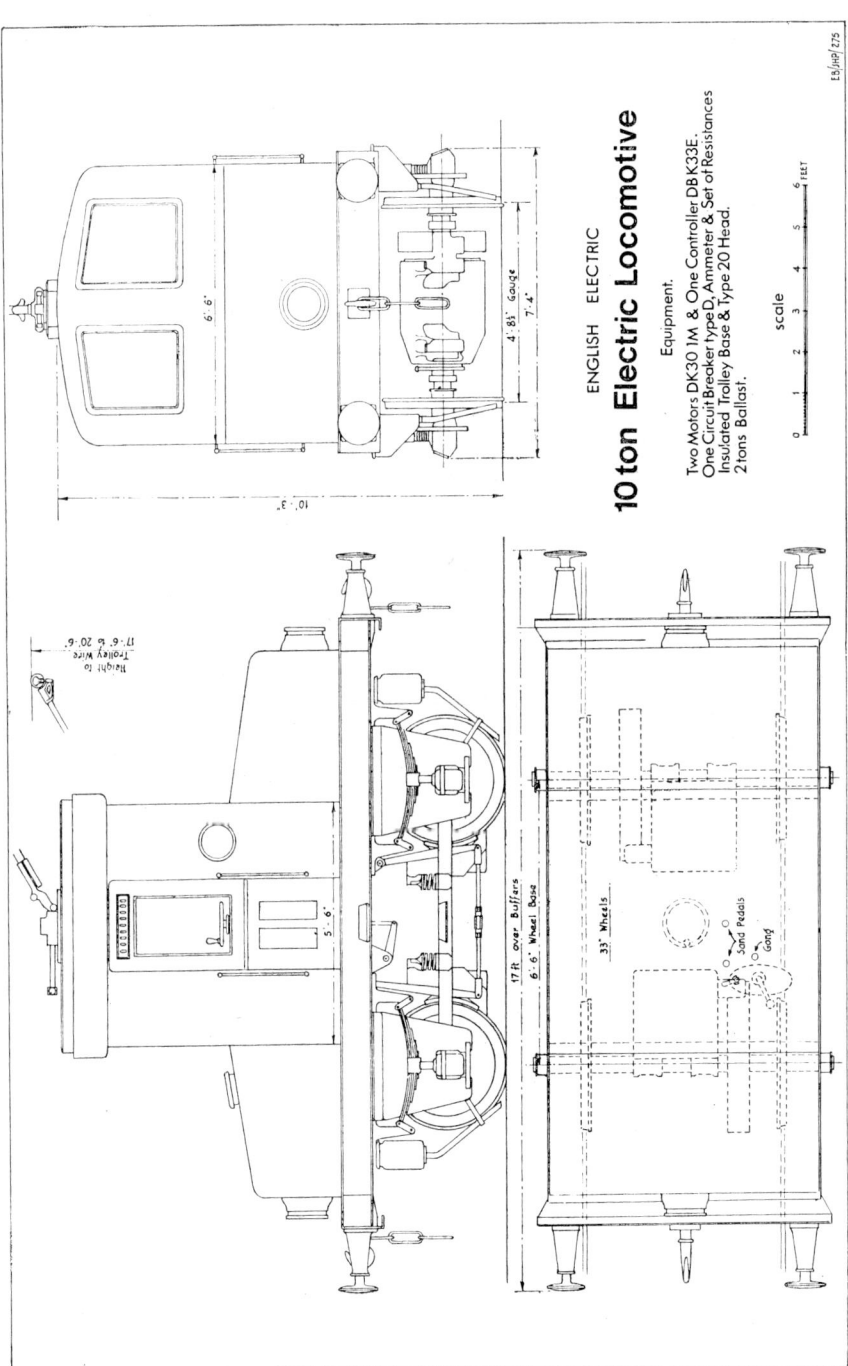

borough, and Thornton Council was ideally placed to extract the maximum advantage from the Corporation's predicament. The Council could point out the great advantage which would accrue to the district if the railway branch line were built, since Cleveleys was suffering from being two miles from the railway. Fearing, no doubt, that opposition from three parties might prove fatal to the Bill and to their scheme for incorporating Thornton, the Corporation accepted an ingenious compromise which satisfied Thornton Council and also released the railways from their branch line proposal, whilst ensuring them a share of the growing traffic from Cleveleys.

The agreed solution was for Blackpool to provide Cleveleys with the facilities which would have been expected from the branch railway line. For passengers, the Corporation would run a bus service from Cleveleys to Thornton Station, and for goods and mineral traffic a service would be provided over the Tramroad from a link with the railway at Copse Road, Fleetwood to sidings which were to be built on the east side of the line just south of Cleveleys station. Neither service was expected to be profitable, but the expense was justified when, on March 18 1919, the railway companies withdrew their Bill for the Cleveleys branch line.

The Blackpool and Fleetwood Tramroad Act of 1896 had forbidden the company to carry any "goods animals or other things" except for luggage and merchandise weighing less than 56 lb which could be carried on the passenger cars. The Company could transport coal or other merchandise for its own use, though, as we saw in a previous section, the facility may not have been used since the early days of the Tramroad, since local cartage had proved cheaper. The Blackpool Improvement Act of 1920 repealed this section of the Tramroad Act, and authorised the goods and mineral service which had been agreed with the railway companies.

The scheme provided for the railway companies to lay down a junction and sidings on the west side of the railway behind Copse Road tram depôt, the cost, estimated at £1300, to be borne by the Corporation. The Corporation would then construct exchange sidings and a line connecting these to the Tramroad, with extra siding accommodation at Cleveleys. Although Cleveleys was intended to be the terminus of the mineral service, the Corporation had the right to run trains as far south as Red Bank Road, Bispham. Since there was no provision in the agreement for any sidings to be built there, the purpose of this clause is a little obscure, unless the intention was to exploit the Corporation's right to carry coal for its own purposes by permitting public sales from Bispham power station. Coal trains would hardly have been popular in Red Bank Road, and after the take-over, the Corporation quickly decided to close the Bispham power station, with the result that the powers to run trains south of Cleveleys were never used.

In view of the cost of providing the new facilities—£30 000 for the mineral service and £20 000 for the Thornton-Cleveleys bus service—the Corporation was in no great hurry. The bus service, the first ever run by the Corporation, began on July 2 1921, but there was no sign of the mineral service. Not until 1924 did work begin on the sidings at Cleveleys, and by then the original site near Cleveleys station was no longer available and the sidings were relocated at Thornton Gate. Work continued in a desultory fashion through 1925 and 1926, although the 1920 Act specified that all powers would lapse if the works were not completed by August 1925; this seems to have been conveniently overlooked.

In 1926 the Corporation was even less enthusiastic about the mineral service than it had been in 1919, and its estimates of the potential traffic convinced the LMS Railway that the proposed exchange sidings at Fleetwood were an extravagance. On July 26 1926, the railway company agreed to postpone construction of the exchange sidings and instead to link the Tramroad directly to the existing Fleetwood Estate Company's siding at the back of Copse Road. This was probably a straightforward reinstatement or reopening of the original link of 1898-9, and would confine exchange traffic to a single track down which wagons would be propelled by one party and taken in tow by the other.

Having thus cut its losses by several thousands of pounds, the Corporation began to prepare in earnest for the new service. In March 1927, a tender was accepted from English Electric for a 10-ton electric locomotive, including 2 tons ballast. What eventually arrived in the summer of 1927 was one of English Electric's standard industrial locomotives, works number 717, identical to a dozen or so others used mainly at power stations, and fitted with two DK 30/1M 50-hp motors and a Dick Kerr controller, with the intention of handling loads of up to 150 tons. It was finished in red with one Corporation crest on each side, and was unnumbered.

The first wagon of coal arrived at Thornton Gate sidings on September 23 1927, more than eight years after the Corporation had agreed to provide the "goods and mineral" service. There is no evidence that any separate goods service was ever operated although, as mentioned in Part 8, the early withdrawal of Box car 101 in 1926 suggests that it might have been intended for some use such as handling passengers' luggage in advance. The Thornton Gate sidings were laid out solely as a coal depot, with two tracks each alongside paved roadways, separate wagon and dray weighbridges, and a coal order office. The total capacity of the yard was quoted as 45 wagons.

The working of the coal trains was rather less sophisticated than had been originally intended, since the absence of the exchange sidings at Fleetwood meant that any shunting had to be carried out at Thornton Gate. Operations, at least in later days, followed a daily routine. The locomotive was shedded at Copse Road, and each morning it would pick up from the siding behind the depôt the loaded wagons, usually not more than six, which had been left there by the LMS earlier in the day. From the siding the locomotive would make its way round the side of the depôt to the front yard, where it would wait until a service car to Blackpool arrived. Once the service car was out of the way, the locomotive would emerge on the main line and make its way slowly down towards Thornton Gate, taking about 15-20 minutes to cover the 2.5 miles. The wagons, being loose-coupled, clattered backwards and forwards noisily as the train slowed for the road crossings, and usually spilled part of its load on to the track, where it was carefully picked up by the local residents.

Above: Thornton Gate coal sidings in 1928, with the Blackpool electric locomotive in its original red livery and coal wagons for the Cleveleys coal merchants.
(Dr Hugh Nicol

Below: Thornton Gate sidings to-day, now serving as Blackpool Corporation's permanent way yard. The bogies used to carry rails are those of a former Tramroad trailer of 1898.
(B. R. Turner

Because of the careful pace at which the loaded trains travelled, the following service car had usually caught up by Rossall, and unwary passengers sometimes received quite a shock when they came up behind a full-size railway train. At Thornton Gate the trains ran past the sidings and then reversed in from the south. There was ample track in the sidings for the locomotive to shunt the wagons into the appropriate positions. In the afternoons the locomotive returned to Fleetwood with the empty wagons. Because of the simple layout at Copse Road there was no facility there for the locomotive to run round the wagons, and therefore the train had to be pushed all the way from Thornton Gate with a flagman stationed on the front wagon, signalling to the driver with red and green flags. Unfortunately, no one seems to have recorded this operation on film.

As the Corporation expected, the service proved to be quite uneconomic, the receipts from freight charges barely sufficing to pay the cost of running the sidings, let alone the cost of haulage and the loan charges. However, they stuck it out until the loan on the locomotive was repaid in 1943, but as soon as postwar conditions allowed the service was closed down, and coal wagons for Cleveleys were left at Thornton railway station. The last coal train ran over the Tramroad on April 30 1949.

The electric locomotive was now redundant, and the Manager, Walter Luff, offered the vehicle to the Light Railway Transport League for preservation. Not unnaturally, the League's Museum Committee had to refuse this offer, since there were more worthy specimens in need of preservation than what was basically a standard industrial locomotive (a similar offer from the Longendale railway was also declined). It was decided therefore to use the locomotive to tow the salt-water spray car 7, formerly toastrack 161, and the locomotive became part of the Permanent Way fleet, although it never received a PW number, or any other for that matter. It was later fitted with a tramway-type coupling, but otherwise remained in original condition. The red livery in which it had arrived in 1927 survived until the vehicle's only full overhaul, at Rigby Road in February 1938, when it was painted in green with dark green lining. The locomotive's only other repaint at Blackpool came in December 1954, again in green, and by this time it was rarely seen outside Copse Road depôt, though it was sometimes used to deliver consignments of rail for the PW department, the rails being carried as usual on the plate frame bogies from Tramroad trailers 11-13.

Copse Road depôt closed on October 1 1963 and the locomotive was moved down to Bispham depôt. Shortly before this it had made a farewell visit round the back of Copse Road to the very limit of the old connecting track, which was lifted shortly afterwards. The sidings at Thornton Gate, which had been disused since the end of the coal trains, were fitted out as permanent way yard in place of Copse Road, and have also served as a graveyard for withdrawn cars, such as six Standards in 1958, several railcoaches in 1963 and Coronation cars in 1970. The locomotive itself remained at Bispham until 1965, when it was moved to Rigby Road for transfer to Crich, surely the only tramway vehicle to be accepted for preservation 16 years after first being offered.

Five weeks after it began, the coal service was suspended for some days due to the weather. On the evening of October 28 1927, the coast was struck by winds of up to 90 miles/h. The trams continued running, though the drivers on the open-fronted Blackpool cars had to be issued with goggles. At 22.20 hrs, Standard car 28, running from Bispham to Pleasure Beach, was blown over on the Tramroad near St Stephens Avenue. Trams continued running on the northbound track until 12.30, when Fleetwood Box car 107 derailed at the Cabin, completely blocking the line. It was 03.20 before car 28 was cleared from the tracks, the bogies being taken to Blundell Street and the top and bottom decks separately to Bispham depôt.

During the night the storm broke through the sea defences at Fleetwood, inundating the entire town; six people were drowned. The whole Tramroad north of Rossall was under water, and Lord Street was filled with thousands of logs which had floated down from the sawmills at Copse Road. The trackbed was washed away for 150 yards between Rossall and Broadwater, leaving the track completely unusable.

To help in the rescue of marooned residents, thirty rowing boats were sent up from Stanley Park to Rossall, where they were loaded on to tram bogies and pushed along the rails until the water was deep enough for them to float. The first tram did not run until November 3,

Above: From 1927 to 1949 coal wagons were hauled by Blackpool's electric locomotive from Copse Road to Thornton Gate and the empty wagons propelled back after unloading. This 1941 view shows the train waiting at Thornton Gate to follow a northbound tram, while a southbound car passes on the third track.
(W. H. Bett

Centre: After coal service ceased on April 30, 1949, the electric locomotive was used by the permanent way department. This view shows it at Copse Road with a BR van on March 5 1957.
(A. D. Packer

Below: A rare photograph of the locomotive at the end of the connecting track to the railway behind Copse Road depôt. This was the last occasion on which the track was used before being lifted in 1963.
(G. S. Palmer

double track not being restored until the following day.

Meanwhile, freed at last from the political troubles which had bedevilled him for the previous five years, Mr. Furness was now able to spend some money on the Tramroad and put into effect his original intention to purchase new cars. The gradual addition of intermediate stops, as new housing spread along the line, meant that faster cars were needed to maintain the schedule, and during 1927 and 1928 the Milnes and Brill bogies of the older saloons were replaced by the standard "Preston" bogies, most of them with more modern and slightly more powerful motors. The bogies under the Glasshouses were fitted nearer the centre of the car, but no attempt was made to improve the restricted corner entrance which the old bogies had necessitated. The attractive curves of the well-sprung Preston trucks gave the older Box cars quite a fleet-footed air compared with the stolid appearance (and hard-riding performance) of the Milnes plate-frame bogies.

To prepare the way for a new fleet, sample motors of different types were obtained and fitted to various Tramroad cars and, since higher running speeds would make air brakes desirable, these were fitted to the retrucked "Glasshouse" cars, and in 1929 to cars 112-115. Integration with the town system meant that the air brakes were a mixed blessing, for their greatly reduced stopping distance sometimes proved embarrassing on the "integrated" section of route between Bispham and the Pleasure Beach. A nasty rear-end collision occurred on the Tramroad in August 1927 when an air-braked "Glasshouse" stopped suddenly at St Stephens Avenue after a late signal from the guard, and was rammed by a Blackpool toastrack running down the slope from the Cabin.

Experiments were carried out with 50-hp GEC WT28S motors under Box car 102, and these were presumably adjudged suitable, since they were chosen (in a slightly different version designated WT28L) for the ten new trams about to be ordered. But, during 1928, Box car 114 was fitted with an experimental set of newly-introduced BTH 509 D1 motors, which were rated at 70 hp and made 114 much the fastest car in the Blackpool fleet, and probably the most powerful single-deck tram in the country. Car 114 has been preserved by the TMS, and is currently in store at Clay Cross; according to the museum stock list it is fitted with GE 67 motors, but there is good reason to believe that the car still in fact retains its high-speed 1928 equipment. Certainly its performance on the Tramroad after restoration as Box car 40 in 1960 caused eyebrows to be raised in several quarters, where the potential of the works car's unusual motors had long been forgotten. Unfortunately, the situation of the car in Clay Cross and the lack of access due to stored equipment has precluded any examination of the motors.

One more step was deemed to be necessary before the Tramroad would be ready for new and faster trams. The American-type harp trolleys were thought to be unsuited to higher speeds, and the Corporation was considering the use of sliding collectors. The idea was probably implanted by English Electric, who used the Tramroad late in 1925 for brief trials with a Fischer bow collector and with an industrial-type Brecknell Munro pantograph fitted with a top roller. In May 1927, Mr. Freddie Field, the Blackpool Tramways Engineer, joined a study group touring the Continent to investigate European methods of current collection, and on his return the Tramways Committee agreed that the new Fleetwood cars should be fitted with sliding collectors. Experiments were carried out with bow collectors and pantographs on double-deck and single-deck cars—thought to have been a Standard car and a Glasshouse—reputedly under the personal aegis of the inventor, Herr Fischer. The trials showed that the bow collector performed unsatisfactorily in strong winds, and accordingly it was decided that the new cars would be fitted with Brecknell Munro and Rogers pantographs using Fischer sliding pans and balance-weights. This decision must have meant changing to non-fouling ears on the overhead, but unfortunately the entire pantograph episode is very poorly documented and no photographs appear to exist of any of the trials which were carried out.

In 1928, a few months after this photograph was taken at the Dickson Road terminus, Fleetwood Box car 114 was fitted with 70-hp BTH 509 motors and became the fastest car in the Blackpool fleet. 114 later became a works car and, after restoration in 1960 as Blackpool and Fleetwood 40, is now preserved by the TMS at Clay Cross.   (Dr H. A. Whitcombe, courtesy Science Museum

Part 10: Fleetwood's posh new trams

ON July 30 1928, the long-suffering residents of Fleetwood witnessed the arrival of the first new design of saloon tram to appear in their streets for almost 30 years. The new tram was Blackpool Corporation 167, the first of a batch of ten cars ordered from English Electric at £2000 each specifically for the Talbot Road—Fleetwood route. They were, in fact, natural descendants of the Tramroad Company saloon cars and, since they were virtually the only modern interurban-style cars to run in Great Britain, they deserve a chapter to themselves. The ten cars were numbered from 167 to 176.

According to 'Tramway and Railway World' for October 18 1928, which gave a comprehensive description of the new cars, the outline specification was prepared by Charles Furness, but all detailed design work was completed by English Electric. It would be interesting to know just how much of the final design was specified by Blackpool and how much was left to Preston's initiative, for the completed vehicle was an intriguing amalgam of urban, interurban, British, American and even continental influences.

Whatever the antecedents, the new trams were among the most elegant vehicles ever to grace a British tramway.

Ever since the new cars were first planned at the time of the take-over in 1920, they had been labelled by the Corporation as "Pullmans", an epithet which during the 1920's was attached fairly indiscriminately to any vehicle whose interior fittings exceeded the absolute minimum of comfort. Tramway operators were particularly prone to delusions in this respect, and the London County Council's much-publicised "Pullman" refurbishing programme of 1926 brought the following comment from the 'Blackpool Gazette & Herald':

"The Blackpool trams, and particularly the latest models, are as comfortable as any to be found in the country, and Londoners would probably go wild with delight were their own trams so comfortably appointed as the latest blue cars of Lytham St Annes. No one who remembers the type of tramcar in use thirty years ago can say that there has been no improvement in design."

Above: One of the Lytham "Pullmans" (41-50) built by English Electric in 1924 and fitted on both decks with reversible two-and-one tilting seats with leather upholstery. At the time, they were perhaps the most comfortable trams in Britain, and caused unfavourable comparisons with the wooden-seated Fleetwood cars. This view shows Lytham 43 outside the depôt in Squires Gate Lane on August 6 1933, in the new livery introduced in that year.
(R. Elliott

Centre: The spacious interior of Blackpool Pantograph car 172, photographed in Bispham depôt. The width of 7ft 6in permitted double reversible seats on each side of the aisle.
(M. Marshall

Below: The first of the class, car 167, was soon fitted with normal end destination boxes in place of the route letters. This view shows 167 reversing outside Talbot Road station with "Glasshouse" 116 and a Box car in the background.
(Dr Hugh Nicol

Presumably this note was penned by one of the Gazette's St Annes reporters, for residents of Bispham, Cleveleys and Fleetwood had no need to cast their minds back; they were able to travel every day on precisely the type of tramcar in use thirty years before, and they were beginning to wonder whether they would have to suffer the primitive garden seats of the hard-riding Tramroad saloons for another thirty years. Visitors, too, were beginning to look twice before committing themselves to a half-hour journey on wooden seats. The 1920's had seen an unprecedented demand for comfort by the travelling public, stimulated by the introduction of luxury motor coaches. The old solid-tyred *chars-à-banc*, which had been the Tramroad's main rival for day excursion traffic, were rapidly being replaced by comfortable new saloons; by 1927 some 200 motor *chars-à-banc* were operating from Blackpool, and of these only 20 still had solid tyres.

The murmurings of discontent were given official weight in June 1927, when Fleetwood Council's licensing committee made its annual inspection of trams and buses. They were struck more than ever by the contrast between the luxury of the motor buses and coaches which they examined and the spartan simplicity of the 39 Tramroad cars which represented Fleetwood's main contact with the outside world in those days before the completion of the direct Blackpool—Fleetwood road. The licensing committee wrote to Charles Furness, pointing out that better things had been expected of the Corporation take-over, and drawing unflattering comparisons with the new Lytham St Annes cars. This was a little unfair, since the Lytham "Pullmans" were some of the most luxurious vehicles ever to run on a British tramway, but the complaint had the desired effect. The Blackpool manager replied that improvements to the Fleetwood rolling stock were being planned at that very moment.

We have already followed the experiments with motors and new forms of current collection which were carried out before the design of the new cars was finalised. The most obvious fruit of these experiments was the use on all ten cars of a Brecknell, Munro & Rogers pantograph (with Fischer pan) mounted on an impressive tower, and it was this feature which gave the cars their permanent nickname. The official title of "Pullman" failed to stick, and it was as "Pantographs" that the new cars became known.

In fact the upholstered seats in the Pantograph cars were identical with those in the lower saloons of the standard cars, the only difference being that they were arranged in double transverse pairs. This arrangement was made possible by building the cars to the extreme width of 7 feet 6 inches, the maximum permitted by the Ministry of Transport and only practicable on lines with widely-spaced tracks and easy curves. The Pantographs were eight inches wider than the lower deck of the Standard double-deckers, and two inches wider than the old Box cars; the impression of unusual width was accentuated by the form of the dash and by its division into two horizontal bands of red and white. The placing of the car number below the headlight instead of above it also contributed to the distinctive frontal appearance.

This air of spaciousness was continued on the platforms, which were intended to accommodate passengers' luggage in summer as well as parcels up to 56 lb which were carried under the tramway parcels scheme. One most unusual feature was the fitting of a double seat on each platform, bringing the total seating capacity to a theoretical 48, though passengers were not actively encouraged to ride on the front platform. These platform seats were not upholstered, because the platforms were not fitted with doors. In the best Tramroad tradition the driver was protected from the weather by a full vestibule—a feature which the Corporation still declined to adopt on its own double-deckers—though no windscreen wiper was fitted. In rainy weather the driver had to open the top hinged portion of the windscreen and peer hopefully through the narrow space provided. Drop windows had served the same purpose on the old Box cars.

Also by Brian Turner (with Steve Palmer):
THE BLACKPOOL STORY
140 pages, 150 pictures, A4 size, full-colour cover, cloth bound £4.95

"Fascinating"................... *Manchester Evening News*	from : **Palmer & Turner**
"Entertaining reading"....... *Daily Mirror*	**34 Kings Walk**
"Engaging reading"........... *Lancashire Life*	**Cleveleys**
"Absorbing"..................... *Modern Tramway*	**Lancs.**

The unusual width of the Pantograph cars is well brought out by this shot of passengers boarding 175 at Talbot Road.
(Dr H. A. Whitcombe, courtesy Science Museum

To the student of tramcar architecture the most unusual feature of the car was the roof, which was unlike any ever seen on a British tram, save for the eight "Cradley" type bogie cars of the Dudley and Stourbridge company. Essentially the roof was a clerestory, a type of construction which had generally gone out of favour, but the ends of the clerestory were swept down to form what the Americans termed a "railroad roof", here confined to the length of the main saloon. The use of a clerestory has caused the Blackpool Pantograph cars to be described as some of the last examples of traditional British tramcar design, but if we look more closely at the construction of the main saloon and its roof, we reach a rather different conclusion.

During the 1920's, English Electric, like other tramcar builders, were developing a nice line in bus body-building, and around 1927 several of their single-deck buses began to feature this distinctive clerestory roof, a type of construction not normally associated with motor bus design. The clerestory did provide a fairly sophisticated method of ventilation, and English Electric were well versed in its use since it was a feature of many of the railway vehicles they turned out for export. Blackpool Corporation in fact bought six of these clerestory-roofed buses in 1928, and they bear an uncanny resemblance to the new trams which arrived in the same year. These buses have been described as tram-like in appearance, but really it seems that the reverse is more correct and that the Pantograph cars, like the LUT "Poppy" and the 1960 Blackpool trailers, were partly built on contemporary motor bus construction principles.

Whatever exotic features English Electric might have incorporated into the body design of the new trams, the Corporation kept its feet firmly on the rails by specifying the faithful old "Preston"

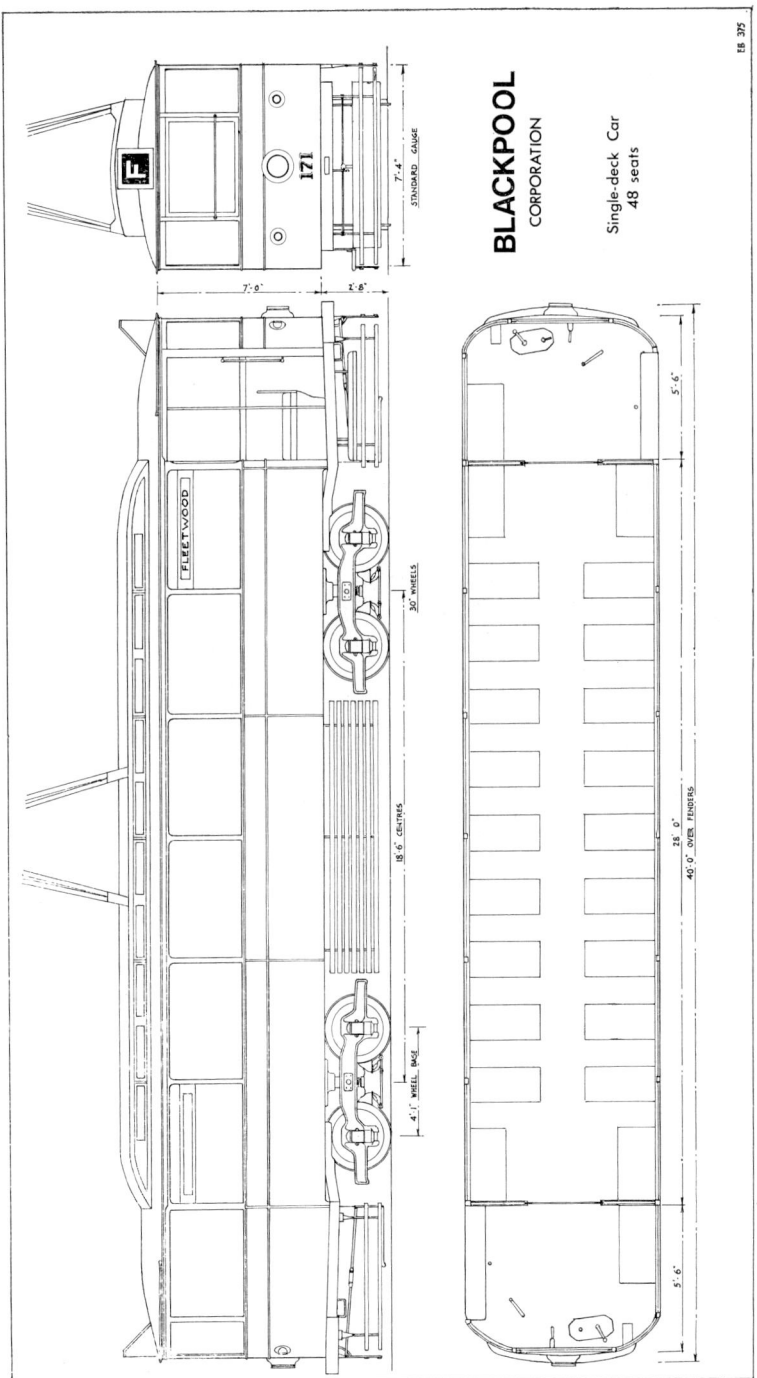

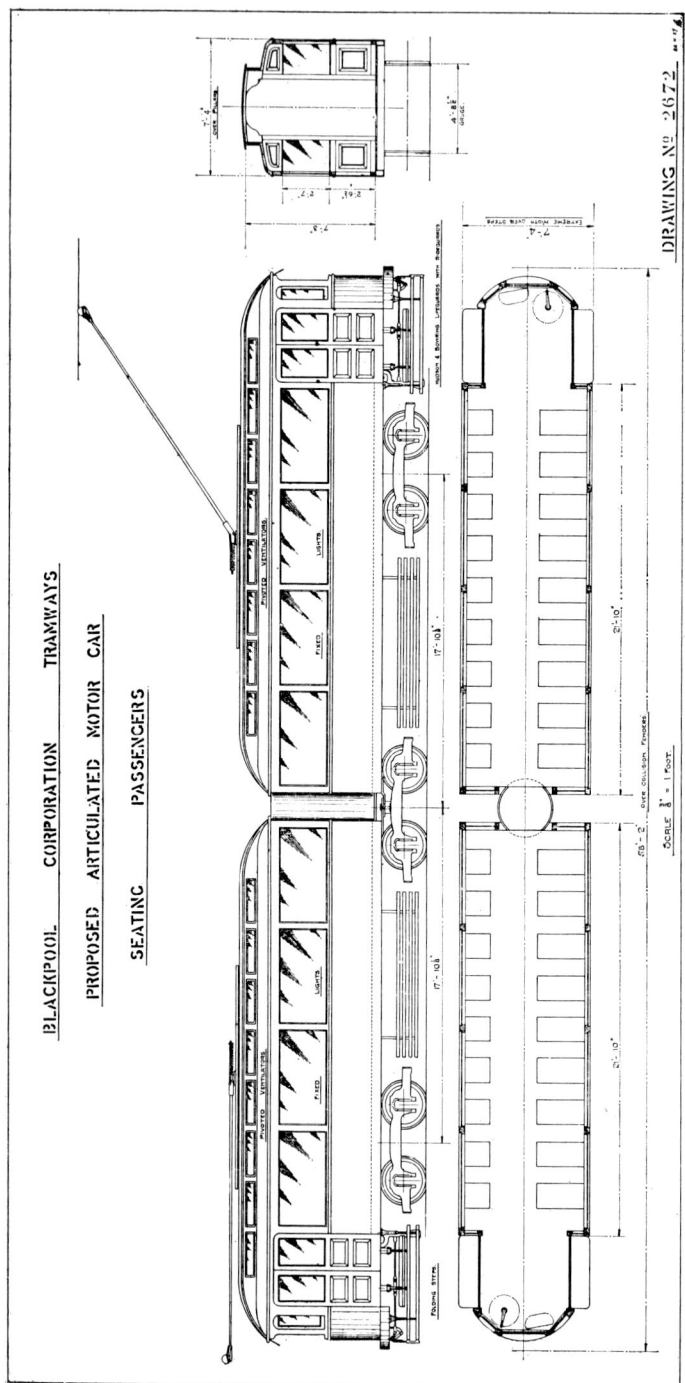

In 1927, Blackpool Corporation and English Electric produced a design for an articulated Blackpool—Fleetwood car, based possibly on the studies then being undertaken for Calcutta. The idea was dropped in favour of the single-unit bogie cars featured on the previous page.

(from 'Blackpool by Tram')

swing-bolster bogies, still the standard Blackpool fitment after almost 20 years. The Corporation and the Tramroad Company had found this bogie tailor-made for the straight and level coastal routes, and it had even been incorporated in an abortive design for an articulated car prepared by the Tramways Department in 1927, presumably with the active support of English Electric. One wonders if any other major British tramway adhered so consistently to one design of bogie over such a long period for so wide a variety of cars.

The high-stepping appearance of the Preston bogies was an important element in the overall aesthetics of the design, aided by the attractive curvature of the clerestory roof and the large saloon windows with their radiussed upper corners. The only jarring notes were struck by the driver's windscreen, which had a slightly home-made look about it, and the crude route-letter box mounted on the roof. This was of the same pattern as the makeshift affairs added to the Fleetwood cars and the single-deck buses after the bus routes had been numbered in 1927.

Intelligent indication of the car's destination was left to the side blinds, whose wording was a constant reminder, right down to 1961, of the line's interurban origin. The Pantograph blinds, which remained exclusive to the Talbot Road—Fleetwood route, contained the following evocative displays: ALL STATIONS TO FLEETWOOD, ALL STATIONS TO BLACKPOOL, STOPPING CAR TO BISPHAM, NORBRECK CLEVELEYS AND FLEETWOOD, ALL STAGES TO CLEVELEYS, FLEETWOOD ONLY, SPECIAL TO FLEETWOOD, ENGAGED CAR, GYNN ONLY, 1. Just how far these displays reflected the operation of the Fleetwood route in 1928 is debatable, for there is no official record of any sort of express service, and in any case it is not clear whether FLEETWOOD ONLY and GYNN ONLY were intended for express runs or merely for local short-workings; the subtlety of ALL STAGES TO CLEVELEYS as against ALL STATIONS is equally mysterious. In view of the fact that there were no less than four alternatives for Fleetwood-bound cars whilst trams in the opposite direction could only show ALL STATIONS TO BLACKPOOL it seems more likely that variation in the northbound displays was a trick played on Blackpool visitors by the inspectors at Talbot Road station on the arrival of a busy train, to persuade the intending passengers to distribute themselves over two or more trams instead of crowding on to the first one. Once out of sight, the "express" car probably behaved just like any other, though

Blackpool Pantograph car 173 at Fleetwood Ferry in 1931, in original condition and red livery.
(M. J. O'Connor, block courtesy TMS

any evidence to the contrary would be welcome.

If some form of express working was intended, the new cars' equipments would be able to provide it, for each Pantograph car had two GEC WT28L 50-hp motors against the 35-hp motors of most of the older tramroad cars. These motors were fitted on the inside axle (one motor per truck) and were outside-hung. The controllers were of type BTH B510, and the cars were fitted with air brakes by the Consolidated Brake Co Ltd, incorporating a conductor's emergency valve.

No 167, the first of the new trams, arrived from Preston at the end of July 1928 and was prepared for service at Rigby Road works. On the morning of July 30, the new car was towed through the town by one of the old Box cars (presumably because the overhead was not suitable for pantograph collectors) and driven up to Fleetwood to be inspected by the licensing committee. With nice regard for municipal boundaries, 167 took the Fleetwood councillors and Press for a run as far as Rossall and back, including an emergency stop to demonstrate the new air brakes. The 'Gazette & Herald', under the heading "Fleetwood's Posh New Trams" commented favourably on the upholstered seats, and said that tramway travel on the route would in future be pleasant instead of painful.

Fleetwood passengers soon began to wonder whether the appearance of car 167 had been an apparition. Throughout August and September the new cars continued to arrive by road from Preston and, one by one, they were stowed away at Rigby Road whilst the faithful Box cars continued to run the Fleetwood service as they had done for the past thirty years. By the end of the 1928 Illuminations the whole class of ten Pantographs had been delivered and still not one of them had turned a wheel in service.

The Tramways Department planned to introduce the new cars for the beginning of the winter service on October 25. This winter schedule of 1928/29 was quite unlike any previously operated in Blackpool; for the first time ever, double-deckers were to be withdrawn from the Promenade route and replaced by a Bispham—Pleasure Beach service operated by the single-deck Box cars from Bispham depôt. Only once before had single-deckers been seen south of Talbot Square in winter when, on January 6 1928, all double-deckers were withdrawn from the Promenade from mid-morning owing to strong winds. This was no doubt to avoid a repetition of the blowing over of car 28 in the previous October.

Unfortunately the first day of the new service dawned still Pantograph-less. The tracks on the curve outside Fleetwood Parish Church were too close to accommodate the overhang of the new cars, and four more days went by before at last the Pantograph class made its debut. At 11.20 on the morning of October 29 1928, tramcar 172 entered service at Cleveleys, and at 15.00 a second car, 176, went on to the road. Two hours later both trams had to be run into Bispham depôt with pantograph trouble, but next day two of the cars stayed on the route all day, sharing the Fleetwood traffic with five of the old saloons which were operating the basic through service for the very last time.

On October 31 the Pantographs took over. Seven of the new cars, running from Bispham depôt, operated the 12-minute Talbot Road—Fleetwood service together with six of the ex-Company cars, four on Cleveleys and two on Bispham turn-backs. Another seven of the old saloons were running on the Bispham—Pleasure Beach route. The ten Pantograph cars soon naturally became the pride of the system, the first new tramcar design to be introduced for seventeen years and the only relatively modern cars in the Blackpool Corporation fleet. It would have seemed incredible in 1928 that within seven years the entire class would be put into store.

Part 11: 1928 to 1932

THE arrival of the ten Pantograph cars in 1928 brought about several significant changes in the operation of the Blackpool tramways — hardly surprising, since this was the largest single influx of new trams since 1902. The most important, and the most permanent, of these changes was in the working of the Promenade service.

For almost 30 years the Tramways Department had been plagued by the problem of operating the Promenade route in winter, when the patronage fell to a fraction of its summertime level. The Corporation's tram fleet was geared largely to seasonal demands, and this meant that for seven months of each year the double-deckers on the seafront were running almost empty. Now at last the Department had surplus rolling stock of just the right capacity for the Promenade. On October 25 1928 seven Fleetwood

The Fleetwood saloons spent their last years on Preston swing-bolster bogies of the type adopted as standard for Blackpool. From 1928 to 1933-4 the Box cars (102-115) ran most of the winter service on the Promenade, returning each summer to the Fleetwood route. These views show retrucked six-window Box car 110 at the Pleasure Beach in June 1933 with a Lytham car behind, and retrucked Glasshouse car 121 at the Pleasure Beach in 1931.
(TMS and
M. J. O'Connor

Box cars, displaced from Dickson Road by the new Pantograph fleet, inaugurated the single-decker winter Promenade service which has prevailed right down to the present day.

At first the Box cars ran only between Bispham and the Pleasure Beach, with no service at all on the new South Promenade extension. Gradually, as housing development began, the winter service was extended to Harrowside, and eventually, by 1933, along the full length of the reservation to Clifton Drive (Starr Gate). None of this was entirely new territory for the Box cars, of course, but the use of Fleetwood vehicles on an internal Blackpool service marked another stage in the gradual integration of the Fleetwood Tramroad.

The new service had one particularly interesting feature. Before the morning rush hour the Promenade route south of Manchester Square was left unserved and the early morning journeys were operated instead to Squires Gate. Each morning, Box cars made nine runs down to Squires Gate—the only recorded occasions when Tramroad cars operated away from the Promenade or Dickson Road—but since the last saloon was safely back on the reservation before 08.00, nobody ever seems to have photographed a Fleetwood car on Lytham Road.

During the 1920's South Shore residents had grown accustomed to the upholstered seats of the Standard cars and the luxurious Lytham Pullmans, and they reacted with dismay when they found themselves having to clamber on board the old wooden-seated Box cars. South Shore councillors were always sensitive about any slight imposed upon them from what they considered to be the more favoured northern end of the town, and their champion in this instance, Coun Halstead, found an added objection to *"these relics from the Fleetwood route"*. Councillor Halstead was in the habit of of walking his dog along the seafront and returning with it on top of the tram—dogs could travel free upstairs. But now, as he put it, *"if you take a dog in one of of those disreputable cars you have to pay threepence for it"*. Under pressure, the Tramways Department had to waive this bye-law on single-deckers operating south of Manchester Square.

The chairman of the Tramways Committee, Alderman Tom G. Lumb, defended the use of the Box cars on the grounds that they were faster and "easier-running" and that many passengers preferred them. They also provided the Promenade drivers with shelter from the elements, but nobody seemed greatly concerned about that. Ald. Lumb was, of course, none other than the Tom G. Lumb who had helped Ben Sykes establish the Fleetwood Tramroad 30 years earlier and had personally drawn up the detailed plans of the line. His enthusiasm for the Tramroad as the catalyst for the development of the coast remained undimmed. By now he was one of Blackpool's most distinguished citizens, and this and his experience of tramways — he had also been engineer to the Blackpool St. Annes and Lytham Company — were to stand the Tramroad in good stead during the 1930's.

The Tramways Committee, no doubt anticipating a degree of consumer-resistance to the use of the Box cars, had already decided, on September 24 1928, to modernise the interiors of the ten oldest cars, 102-111. The oppressive interior partition was removed and the wooden garden seats replaced by the standard Blackpool pattern of moquette upholstery. The width of the cars allowed transverse seats for 44 passengers, only four less than the Box cars had previously accommodated. Curiously the four newest saloons, 112-115, retained their wooden seats for another five years.

In summer the Box cars returned to the Fleetwood route, running either to Talbot Road or to South Shore. The addition of the ten new saloons meant that the open crossbench cars were seen much less frequently than in previous years. Now they appeared only at the height of the season and during warm weather. To some extent this was a sign of the times, for public taste was moving away from open trams with wooden seats, and the refreshing breeze which had been so welcome in the days of voluminous Edwardian fashions was now regarded more as an unpleasant draught. But there were still those who hankered after the traditional ride to Fleetwood, and the 'Gazette & Herald' recorded the sad experience of two of them, waiting at the Gynn for an open car to appear:

"Tramcar after tramcar labelled 'All Stations to Fleetwood' passed us. Some had the usual trolley poles. Some had the more artistic pantograph current-collector. Some cars were painted red; some were painted brown. Some had upholstered seats; some had hard wooden ones. But every car was covered in, top and sides. And it was a very hot day.

"Now and again a 'Dreadnought' double-decker with open top would pass

us, and now and again one of the Promenade open toastracks. But these cars were only going to Bispham and we wanted to go to Fleetwood.

"We waited and waited and waited. But no open car appeared. At five o'clock we went home for tea."

One of the most pressing problems caused by the delivery of the Pantographs was that of depôt space. The passenger fleet now totalled 157 vehicles and the three running sheds could hold only 140. The Tramways Committee had approved a scheme to extend Bispham depôt to accommodate the new cars; this would have been the third extension of the shed, the last being in 1914 when the four newest Box cars were delivered. Second thoughts then prevailed and it was decided instead to build a new depôt at Rigby Road to act as a summer overflow for the adjacent Blundell Street shed. This new building, which is now the tramway workshops, was opened in 1929 and was connected to the car works traverser. Four of the Fleetwood cars were presumably transferred to this new depôt during the summer of 1929, for only 43 of the 47 single-deckers were being operated by Bispham.

In 1930, all the Fleetwood cars were back under Bispham's control and, as the depôt in Red Bank Road could accommodate 40 cars, we must assume that the remainder were shedded at Copse Road, Fleetwood. In all probability, some of the open cars were transferred there permanently in 1928 to make room at Bispham for the Pantographs. During the winter they would be able to earn their keep occasionally as works cars, and one crossbench car at each of the Tramroad sheds would be fitted with the big V-shaped snowploughs which the Company had used on those rare occasions when the Fylde Coast experienced any snow worth ploughing.

From 1928 to 1933 Bispham depôt was busier than it had ever been. In winter a minimum of 17 cars was turned out every day—seven on Talbot Road—Fleetwood, four on Talbot Road—Cleveleys and six on the Promenade, whilst in summer the service reached a maximum of 27 cars — 14 on Fleetwood, four on Cleveleys and nine on the Promenade, with the rest of the single-deck fleet working special journeys. In 1932, congestion outside the awkwardly-situated depôt grew so bad that six open cars had to be transferred to Blundell Street on August 5 to operate Promenade specials.

There were three casualties amongst the Fleetwood cars during this period. Two disappeared during the winter of 1928-9 and another in 1930-1. They were all ex-Yankee cars: 117, 118 and 122, but it is not certain in which order they were withdrawn, nor what happened to them, though a tantalising Tramways Committee minute of April 27 1929 records sanctioning £150 for *"conversion of an electric tram car as a loco van for haulage of road material on tram track"*. This presumably refers to a Tramroad vehicle, since the road under construction paralleled the tramroad, and by 1929 this function on the town system would be performed by Highways Department lorries. At this stage of research, unfortunately, the works

Retrucked Box car 104 at North station (Talbot Road) terminus, after removal of the central saloon partition. (TMS

car fleet between the wars is still shrouded in mystery, and any information from readers would be particularly welcome.

For the rest of the Fleetwood vehicles, the years between 1929 and 1933 saw few changes. Five of the crossbench cars were fitted with coloured lights round their side valances for the 1930 illuminations, and operated evening specials between Cleveleys and the Pleasure Beach; otherwise the only significant alteration was the fitting of full destination boxes on all the Fleetwood cars early in 1932, displacing the enigmatic route letters.

There was an odd sort of inertia about the running of the Fleetwood route and, indeed, the entire Blackpool system at this time. Attention was being focussed more and more upon the ailing motor bus services, which were threatening to dissipate the entire profits earned by the trams. In 1930, for instance, the trams earned £21 933 profit on receipts of £321 703, whilst the buses lost no less than £16 883 on receipts of only £67 037.

Buses posed a double problem for the Transport Committee (as it was designated after 1929), and they spared no effort to protect the Tramroad's share of the Blackpool—Fleetwood traffic from the possibility of motor bus competition.

When the line had been built, the route chosen lay well away from existing roads but, soon after the turn of the century, the Estate Companies, who owned much of the land over which the Tramroad passed, began to construct roads alongside the line. From the Gynn to Norbreck and from Cleveleys to Rossall these roads were complete by around 1905, and the Tramroad Company had power to lay their line in the road along the cliffs, if coast erosion threatened the sleeper track. There remained two substantial gaps, involving lengthy detours for road traffic, and this served to maintain the Tramroad's monopoly of the direct Blackpool —Fleetwood route right up to 1930.

On April 22 of that year, the new "Broadway" was opened between Rossall and Fleetwood and, on March 24 1932, the final link in the direct road was completed with the opening of the Norbreck—Anchorsholme section. By this time, though, the Corporation had contrived to safeguard their monopoly of the regular Blackpool — Fleetwood traffic. They had already bought out the local Fleetwood bus service, operated by Councillor William Smith, on August 14 1926, and in May 1929 had combined this with their Blackpool—Thornton route to provide the first through bus route to Fleet-

Five of the Fleetwood crossbench cars were fitted in 1930 with coloured lights for use as illuminations specials. They included car 132, seen here at Copse Road after withdrawal. (M. J. O'Connor

wood, by the "back route", with a running time of 39 minutes, only one minute longer than the trams. Thus ensconced, Blackpool could claim to be the "established operator" under the future provisions of the 1930 Road Traffic Act, but motor *chars-à-banc* continued to make inroads into the Fleetwood excursion traffic, and in September the Corporation introduced an express bus service running on Fleetwood Market Days at a fare of one shilling return, the same as the trams.

During 1931, discussion took place between the Corporation, Ribble Motor Services and the LMS Railway with a view to co-ordinating their operations within the area, and the result was that, while the Corporation retained their monopoly of the Blackpool — Fleetwood service, Ribble took most of the local traffic, including the pioneer Cleveleys—Thornton bus service which the Corporation relinquished, without much regret, on December 20 1931.

It must have become clear by this time that Charles Furness, who was due to retire shortly, was not the man to revitalise the flagging Transport Department, and in November 1931, with surprisingly little public controversy, the decision was made to appoint a new Transport Manager. The change was arranged with commendable diplomacy. Charles Furness was to remain as Borough Electrical Engineer, though this post was a comparative sinecure since the town now obtained 90 per cent of its electricity from Preston Corporation's new generating station at Penwortham. To preserve Mr Furness' pension rights, his salary of £1600 as Electrical and Transport Manager was maintained, £1250 being allocated to his services as Electrical Engineer and the balance made up as "Illuminations duties". In addition to this, Mr Furness would be available to act as "Consulting Transport Engineer" when required. It was all very civilised, and a welcome change from the manner in which the manager had been treated some years earlier.

The Corporation then set about advertising for a Transport Manager, with the declared brief that his first function would be to report on the reorganisation of the system. But not even the most radical member of the Council could have been prepared for quite such a whirlwind of reorganisation as was about to descend on the Blackpool Corporation Transport Department.

Part 12: The new broom

WHEN Charles Furness left the Blackpool Transport Department on December 31 1932, exactly 13 years had passed since the Blackpool & Fleetwood Tramroad Company came under Corporation control. During that period the integration and development of the Fleetwood line had progressed at a pace which might be charitably described as "steady". Before we pass on to the next phase in the story of the Tramroad, we will pause briefly to consider the state of the line. How much had it changed after 13 years of municipal management?

On the rolling stock side, not a great deal. The basic Talbot Road—Fleetwood service was now provided by the new Pantograph cars, but there were still 36 of the original 41 Company cars running each summer, most of them over 30 years old. Of the 19 crossbench cars (123-141) all but car 139 survived—many of them still with their original equipment. The main casualties had been amongst the semi-open "Yankee" cars (116-122) of which only 116, 119, 120 and 121 survived as enclosed "Glasshouses".

More surprising was the fact that 14 out of the 15 "Box" saloons (101-115) were still running on the Promenade and Fleetwood routes. Many of these cars had been in almost daily use since 1899, and it might have been expected that other casualties would follow car 101 once the Pantographs were delivered. Instead the ten oldest cars had been refurbished with upholstered seats and new bogies and several also received new motors, though cars 104, 106, 107 and 111 retained their original GE 1000 equipment.

The most obvious changes had taken place in the permanent way, and a ride along the line would have demonstrated several major improvements. Leaving Talbot Road, the most obvious of these was the smooth exit along the relaid Dickson Road where once the Tramroad cars had scuttled from loop to loop over the single track. At the end of the street, the Gynn, once the nerve-centre of Fleetwood operations in summer, was no longer a point of any operating significance for the Tramroad. Most of the summer Specials were now through-routed with the Promenade, and extra service cars could run through to Talbot Road without difficulty. Even the elaborate 1924 third-track layout was little used.

From the Gynn to Bispham the route had changed character noticeably, being now part Tramroad and part Promenade route. A new station had been built at Bispham a few yards north of the old building in 1932, the only one of the old Company stations to be replaced by a new building of equivalent status. The line down Red Bank Road to Bispham depôt now appeared as an orthodox single-track street tramway, since the Corporation had taken over and paved the old Tramroad-owned private road in 1923.

The track layout at Bispham station had not changed from Company days, although during the Illuminations this was now the busiest point on the whole system. Dreadnoughts, toastracks and Standard cars from the Promenade reversed there regularly, and on October 15 1931, 29 of the Lytham open-toppers had been hired and operated through to Bispham on Lights specials; this became a regular occurrence until the blue cars finished in 1937. The ultimate in Bispham activity was reached on the evening of October 4 1933, when no less than 92 fully-loaded trams were despatched southwards in one hour, *"using special means of turning the trolley poles"*.

Between Cabin and Norbreck the east side of the Tramroad was now protected by the precast concrete fencing which was soon to become a trademark of the Fleetwood route, but otherwise there was little change between Bispham and Rossall save that the parallel road now continued along the whole of this length, whilst at Cleveleys the bucolic station with adjacent hedgerows had disappeared beneath Victoria Square. An unattractive shelter of the Promenade style had replaced the old station building in 1930. At Rossall the old station building had been re-erected when the line was diverted in 1925, whilst the scene in Fleetwood had changed completely from Company days, with the removal of the setts and the centre poles and the extension round the Pharos St lighthouse, which had severed the connexion to the old depôt in Bold Street.

Many of these improvements had helped to speed up the operation of the Fleetwood route, but this had been largely offset by the increasing number of intermediate stops as housing developed between the main stations. Journey times had been reduced slightly since the takeover, and the 10-minute service of 1932 required only eight cars, one less than in 1920. For most of the 1920's, the basic service between Talbot Road and Fleetwood had called for seven cars on a 12-minute headway, not a great improvement on the six-car 15-minute service which the Company had provided for most of its existence. Journey times now varied between 35 and 38 minutes for the eight miles, depending on season and time of day.

On the whole, there was not an enormous amount to show for 13 years of municipal ownership, and it was no surprise that the Fleetwood Tramroad was one of the prime targets in the Five Year Plan for the reorganisation of the Transport Department. This modernisation scheme was drawn up by the new Transport Manager, Mr Walter Luff, and included the introduction of a radically new type of tramcar which he had designed specifically for the Fleetwood route.

That at least is what official histories would have us believe. There is little documentary evidence to contradict it, but there are several reasons for doubting the official line. For one thing, the Corporation had already declared its intention to reorganise the system when the splitting of the Transport and Electricity functions had been agreed at the end of 1931. Something obviously had to be done to replace the ageing Fleetwood cars and, since the Five Year Plan was destined to eradicate the ex-Company cars, perhaps this is an appropriate moment at which to look more closely at the background to the reorganisation.

The financial results of the late 1920's and early 1930's were causing growing concern to the Corporation. Tramway receipts were virtually static, even declining slightly under the impact of the Depression — Blackpool's tram profits always tended to reflect the prosperity of the textile industry. Capital investment had almost dried up after the heavy expenditure on track, cars and workshops in the previous decade, but it was obvious that something would soon have to be done to replace the antiquated rolling stock which provided summer service on the Fleetwood and Promenade routes. Replacement by buses had been a popular

Blackpool 200, the prototype car, photographed early in 1933 on English Electric's test track at Preston. (GEC-AEI

Scenes on the Preston works test track

In 1929, English Electric built an experimental single-deck tram, No. 757, for Liverpool Corporation, mainly to provide a test vehicle for what are now known as monomotor bogies (one motor in each truck driving both axles). The Blackpool 1928 cars served as the basis for the body design, though with shortened platforms. (English Electric Co Ltd.

theme in the mid-'twenties, but the arguments of the bus lobby had been completely discredited by the appalling financial results of the new bus services.

The Corporation thus had little alternative to modernising the seafront tramway, and this decision must have been reached, though not expressly announced, in 1931 when Charles Furness' departure was agreed. His successor, it was stated in April 1932, would report on the proposed reorganisation of the Transport Department. On the face of things, there was then a gap of a year before the new manager took office and the reorganisation scheme was prepared. The "authorised version" of the events reads thus:

November 1932—Walter Luff selected as manager.

January 1 1933—Walter Luff takes office.

February 20 1933—Committee approve purchase of new single-deck tram as per model displayed by Mr. Luff.

March 27 1933—Committee approve 26-point reorganisation plan.

April 1 1933—Five Year Plan commences.

June 23 1933—New tram enters service.

June 26 1933—24 more trams ordered.

Even for a man of Walter Luff's prodigious energy, this timetable is beyond credibility. Other hands must have been at work during 1932, both on the modernisation scheme and on the design of the new tram. There is no question of prior involvement by Mr Luff, for his appointment was announced only in November 1932 after the original choice, Mr Charles Hopkins, had been persuaded to remain as manager at Sunderland where, significantly, he had already initiated just such a programme of tramway modernisation as was envisaged for Blackpool. Mr Hopkins himself had not been chosen until October 17, and by that time the essentials of the scheme must have been decided. But who was pulling the strings?

The redoubtable Alderman Tatham, erstwhile champion of the bus faction, was certainly involved at some level. He was determined, according to the 'Gazette & Herald', that there should be a change of transport manager, and, having finally disposed of his old adversary Charles Furness, Alderman Tatham underwent a conversion the like of which had scarcely been seen since St Paul. In a statement in January 1934 which should not necessarily be taken at face value, Alderman Tatham announced *"I have been a scrap-the-trams merchant for fifteen years and now I believe I have changed my mind. I have altered my mind because the man who is now the transport manager of Blackpool is working a revolution in the transport world. I do believe that we shall soon have trams running from Fleetwood to Lytham along the front."*

The man whom Alderman Tatham was later to succeed as Transport Committee Chairman, Alderman Tom G. Lumb, would naturally be involved in any pre-Luff planning, and it is the Chairman who provides a link to what the writer considers is the likeliest source of impetus behind the modernisation—English Electric. The Preston firm had always been closely involved with the Blackpool tramways during Charles Furness' managership, and Alderman Lumb must have enjoyed close relations with the company's senior members since he had worked for many years with the Fleetwood Tramroad, whose directors had founded the original Preston company.

English Electric were concerned at the falling-off of tramcar orders, and their design staff were certainly at work on new ideas aimed at reviving the flagging market. The larger towns generally built their own trams, and Blackpool (which did not) was an obvious sales target. English Electric thus had an obvious interest in Blackpool's Five Year Plan, since they were the most likely builder of the new trams, and there are good reasons to believe that English Electric were hoping to receive the bulk of the bus orders too, but this was thwarted by trade union pressure to patronise the local Burlingham factory. It may be significant that English Electric designed and built the prototype of the famous 1936 streamlined centre-entrance buses, though the rest of the order went to Burlingham.

English Electric's immediate concern was the new tramcar, which Walter Luff announced in his report with a sentence which did little to conceal his opinion of the Fleetwood Box cars: *"It is necessary to obtain new tramcars to replace the box-type narrow-entrance slow-moving cars on the Fleetwood and Bispham section to enable the journey from Blackpool to Fleetwood to be accomplished in 30 minutes"* The origins of the prototype of this new fleet, which became Blackpool No 200, are as clouded as the rest of the Five Year Plan. English Electric declared that the car had been designed by Mr Luff, which is patently absurd in view of the timetable outlined earlier, and can safely be dismissed as a diplomatic courtesy. In fact, the basic design was conceived by Mr. William Lockhart Marshall, car works manager of English Electric at Preston, and the detail design was prepared by Mr R. J. Heathman, Preston's chief designer, who was later responsible for the Liverpool "Green Goddess" cars.

Work on the car must obviously have begun before 1933, and this has given rise to several speculations in the past— that the car was built for South America and diverted to Blackpool, or that it was a demonstration model for Continental buyers and was to go on exhibition in Bruxelles, possibly during a UITP conference. Until some historian can unearth evidence of English Electric's activities at this time, we cannot be certain, but the writer is inclined to discount these theories and accept what English Electric declared in the publicity hand-out—that the car was designed for Blackpool. What the hand-out did not say was that the car was first conceived as a speculation, without any firm order, in the same way as the recent Tyneside prototype by Metro-Cammell.

Examination of the design reveals several features which were tailor-made for operation on the sea-front route— curved glass roof-lights and maximum forward visibility for viewing the Illuminations, sliding-roof for summer tourist traffic, pantograph tower for Fleetwood operation, two-motor equipment in a bogie layout obviously intended for level routes, and a general use of simple, reliable equipment in the best Blackpool tradition. The only discordant feature was the meagre provision for passengers' luggage, which was an important consideration on summer Saturdays.

It seems probable, therefore, that the new trams were designed either in concert with the Corporation in 1932, or independently by English Electric with Blackpool in mind as the potential customer. The second theory is the more likely, for English Electric also built a double-deck prototype with the same features, and may have hoped that this car too would be adopted by Blackpool, though in the event it became Sunderland 99. The new Blackpool tram was not to be unveiled until Guest Week, a Corporation scheme to encourage early-season holidays in June, and until then the details of the design were to be kept secret. On March 3, Walter Luff announced an embargo on the publication of photographs of the tram, although as far as is known, all that existed at that stage was the model; production of the actual prototype did not, it is believed, begin until after the Blackpool order was officially placed on February 20. All this secrecy has very effectively obscured the true origins of the new vehicle.

One feature of the new tram which soon became public knowledge was its colour scheme, the currently popular green and cream. The model which the Committee saw on February 20 had been painted in this livery, and it was decided to adopt this colour scheme for the entire fleet in place of red and white. A simplified version of the old livery had been introduced on several Standard and Fleetwood Box cars in 1932, dispensing with the teak-and-white side panels in favour of red, and simplifying the lining.

The first green tram, believed to be Standard car 28, appeared on the Squires Gate route on March 22 1933, and soon afterwards the Pantograph cars began to emerge from the paint shop in the new livery. Eventually, it is thought, all the Fleetwood crossbench cars were turned out in green and cream, but the Box cars remained in red — a clear indication of their intended demise. A certain amount of amusement was caused in the paint shop by Walter Luff's insistence on referring to the livery as "green and ivory", since the paint tins were quite clearly labelled "cream".

After inspecting the new tram, No 200, in June, the Committee at once authorised the purchase of a further 24, significantly the number estimated as needed to cover the entire service to Fleetwood. The orders were placed with English Electric without the invitation of tenders from other manufacturers, and an attempt to debate this point in the town council in March 1934 was rebuffed by both Alderman Lumb (*"We have had sample trams prepared and built and the estimates have been carefully gone into. These trams have been approved and the contracts placed with a firm of which the whole of the Committee are thoroughly satisfied"*) and the Mayor, Alderman Tatham (*"You cannot compete in this matter; it is specciality work. There is not another firm making trams like ours. They cannot. They are not allowed to. There are patent rights. This is the way we progress in Blackpool."*)

Modernisation of the Fleetwood Tramroad was one of the first priorities of the reorganisation scheme, and the forthcoming improvements were presaged in a Blackpool Corporation advertisement to mark the incorporation of Fleetwood as a borough in 1933. After pointing out the common interest of the two boroughs in the transport service (Fleetwood supplying the electric current, and Blackpool the cars) it read: *"Before the end of 1933 it is expected that a fleet of luxury cars will be in daily use between Fleetwood and Blackpool, and the two towns will then be only 30 minutes apart. The new cars will be speedy, safe and comfortable, well lighted and heated, and will give really good travel; no matter how good or bad the weather may be, the journey between the two towns will be done in absolute comfort."*

Part 13 The eighth wonder of Blackpool

THE Five-Year Plan for the reorganisation of Blackpool's transport began officially on April 1 1933. As far as the tram routes were concerned, the Plan was neatly summarised in two recommendations:

1. To modernise the cars used on the Fleetwood and Promenade route during the next few years, because this route will be a tramway for many years to come.
2. To spend no more money than is necessary for safety on the other tram routes and, when financial circumstances permit, to seriously consider alternative forms of transport.

The sort of "modernisation" that Mr Luff had in mind was indicated in a report he made on the problems of operating Lytham Road cars along the Promenade:

"With rail-borne vehicles it is impossible to ensure an equally-spaced service during rush periods because from Talbot Square to the Manchester Hotel the Squires Gate cars are sandwiched between cars for the Pleasure Beach and, owing to the different types of cars, with different loading and unloading speeds, the slowest car is also the quickest car. Some of the cars cannot be loaded in under two minutes and, when the cars are also carrying a large number of bags, the position is rendered more difficult. The ideal of the department is to have cars which can be loaded in thirty seconds, as is the case with toastracks and the new railcars. Some of the present cars have been in service for many years (more than thirty in a number of cases) and although these cars were at one time entirely suitable, it is now necessary to speed up, because it is neither possible nor economical to multiply the number of cars on a given

"New Box" car 114 at the Pleasure Beach in 1931 on a through working from Fleetwood. The car behind is one of the two 1898 Dreadnoughts.
(Allen & Sons, Blackpool.

section. The new type of car, coupled with the ticket-issuing machine, will, it is believed, go a long way to solving the congestion problem."

It needs little imagination to deduce that the cars which took two minutes to load were the Fleetwood saloons—*"box type, narrow-entrance, slow-moving cars"* as Mr Luff had described them. Not that the Box cars were condemned out of hand. In February 1933 the Transport Committee minutes recorded that *"the Manager reported on a number of single-deck cars in use at present with only narrow entrances, and he received authority to experiment with one of such cars with a view to providing a wider entrance and thus facilitating quicker loading and unloading."*

One suspects that this experiment was suggested by the Committee rather than the Manager, probably because the Box cars had been modernised only four years before. Any attempt to introduce a more orthodox entrance must have encountered severe problems with the positioning of the bogies and the straight-through underframes. No details are known of the work carried out, but it is unlikely that the rebuilt car ever left the works. The vehicle involved was presumably eight-window Box car No 103, which is recorded as being withdrawn in March 1933. The failure of this experiment inevitably sealed the fate of the remaining Fleetwood saloons.

At the same Committee meeting which authorised this rebuilding, the official order was confirmed for the new streamlined tram from English Electric. There can be little doubt about the Committee's intention to place a bulk order, since the price agreed with English Electric for the sample vehicle was precisely £2000 which was no more than the ten Pantograph cars had cost five years earlier. At this price the new tram was, in marketing terms, a "loss leader", and English Electric were clearly expecting to recover their development costs over a large repeat order. The price for production models of the new tram eventually worked out at £2356 each.

Officially the new tram was to be introduced for the Corporation's Guest Week in June, but English Electric had a more significant deadline in mind. On June 21, the 32nd annual conference of the Municipal Tramways & Transport Association was due to commence at the Imperial Hotel, Blackpool, and W. L. 'Mac' Marshall, the guiding light behind the new design, was well aware of the unique opportunity this would give him to demonstrate his new tram before the assembled Managers of every important tramway in the country. At Preston Works, Marshall and his Chief Designer, R. J. Heathman, worked flat out to ensure that the new tram was ready. If, as now seems likely, the new car had not progressed beyond overall drawings before W. L. Marshall sold the idea to Walter Luff early in 1933, then the design and production stages had to be completed in only five months.

The precise delivery date is not recorded, but the new tram made its first appearance in Blackpool at 23.00 on June 19, only 36 hours before the conference was due to begin. In the best tramway tradition, the new car was given its first trial runs along the Promenade under cover of darkness.

The conference was opened by the retiring President, Charles Furness, who was making his last official appearance as a representative of the Transport Department. The new single-decker was parked on the rarely-used loop at Gynn Square during the conference, and the Managers were naturally taken for a tour. W. L. Marshall recalled the Birmingham Manager, Arthur Baker, turning to him during the trip and saying *"I'm sorry, Mac, but you're twenty years too late."*

At 16.00 hours on June 23 1933, the new tram entered public service from Blundell Street shed, running on the Promenade route between Bispham and Harrowside. As if to symbolise the complete break with everything traditional on the Blackpool tramways, it bore the fleet number 200 instead of the expected 178. To visitors from Lancashire and Yorkshire, many of whom had not even seen a Manchester Pilcher or a Leeds Horsfield car, the effect was quite sensational. One elderly resident was so nonplussed by the coach-like interior of the tram that she booked to Newton Drive in the firm belief that she was on a No 5 bus. Inspectors reported that male passengers were removing their hats when boarding the car, and a visitor from Manchester summed it all up by saying *"When you step on it, you look round instinctively for a mat to wipe your feet on."* No smoking or standing was allowed.

Publicity for the new tram was world-wide. One motor manufacturer included a photograph of No 200 along with the racing car 'Bluebird' and an aeroplane, to illustrate the latest techniques in streamlining. Walter Luff himself seemed unimpressed by all the fuss, particularly when the Press referred to No 200 as *"the new super tram".* He replied:

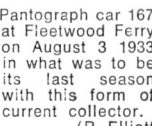
Pantograph car 167 at Fleetwood Ferry on August 3 1933 in what was to be its last season with this form of current collector.
(R. Elliott

"These cars were designed for Blackpool's special conditions and to replace cars which have been in operation for over 30 years, so there are bound to be changes. We do not like the word 'super' attached to them." Nobody seemed inclined to describe No 200 simply as a tram, and references varied from railcar de-luxe to "the eighth wonder of Blackpool" and the inevitable Pullman, but eventually the new design became known as the Railcoach.

No 200 was painted in a variation of the green-and-ivory livery which had been introduced in March 1933 to distinguish the Corporation vehicles from the red Ribble buses which operated the Blackpool—Preston service. Not everybody was enthusiastic about the change, but the 'Gazette' approved it with a verse of doubtful accuracy and scansion:

> Some towns have trams of brown and blue
> And some of red and black.
> And some have trams of yellowish hue
> That send shivers down your back.
> Some paint their cars in stripes and stars
> But the finest I have seen
> Are Blackpool's new creations
> In ivory and green.

Green had, in fact, been used before on the Promenade trams. Precise dates are difficult to establish, but it seems that green and white were the Corporation colours around 1894 and that red panels were added in 1898. Eventually this green and red livery gave way to red, teak and white around 1910. Confirmation of these early liveries would be welcome.

Not everything about the new trams was perfect. Luggage space in the centre entrance was fairly limited, although one census revealed a total of 48 pieces of luggage stacked in the entrance of a railcoach. Space in the main saloon and cabs of No 200 was also restricted. A "daily rider" from Bispham wrote: "A few days ago I had my first and last ride on the so-called super tramcar, and I found that for a person of my height (5 ft 11 in) to sit down properly in such narrow seats was utterly impossible. I had to sit sideways with my legs in the centre passage. For any person above the height of 5 ft 6 in or so, the space between the seats on the new car is much too narrow for comfort and I venture to say that a car where one can neither stand, smoke, nor sit down properly, or take luggage, is useless in a place like Blackpool." The later railcoaches were 2 feet longer than No 200 and this overcame the problem, the extra space being shared between the driving cabs and the saloon.

Official photographs of No 200 at Preston show the car fitted with a pantograph, of a type larger and wider than those fitted to cars 167-176. Whether this pantograph was ever fitted to No 200 at Blackpool is not certain, but it seems unlikely, since only a week later Mr Luff presented a report on the Pantograph cars to the Committee, and shortly afterwards the existing pantographs on cars 167-176 were replaced by trolley poles. So far as is known, the Promenade was never completely adapted for sliding collectors, and the fact that the new car entered service

Above: Bispham in 1905, with crossbench, "Yankee" and saloon cars of the Blackpool and Fleetwood Tramroad Company.
(Commercial postcard courtesy G. L. Gundry

Centre: The same spot thirty years later, with three generations of Fleetwood trams. The acute angle of crossbench car 133's trolley pole contrasts noticeably with that of railcoach 214 and the even shallower angle of Pantograph car 175. In 1937 the Pantograph towers were lowered by 15 inches and those on the railcoaches by some six inches. (TMS

Below: When some older Fleetwood saloons were withdrawn in 1933 their upholstered seats were transferred to the 1914 box cars, No 112-115. This is an interior view of the preserved car 40 (ex-114).
(M. J. O'Connor

on the Promenade route suggests that it must have had a trolley pole from the start. In November 1930, Mr Field, the engineer responsible for the experiments in current collection, remarked that it would be a relatively simple matter to convert the Promenade route to bow-collector operation, but that it had not been found practicable anywhere to employ the collector on an open-deck car, and that as the Lytham St Annes cars used the Promenade track and were not fitted with the collector, the change was not likely to be effected. This does not explain the sudden conversion of 167-176, on which point the official records are silent.

Mention of the Lytham St Annes cars raises another railcoach mystery—the legendary trip to Lytham which had to be abandoned when the car derailed on a right-angle curve at Ansdell. This occasion is so firmly rooted in tramway folklore that it seems sacrilegious to cast doubt upon it, but the writer has been unable to find any documentary evidence to suggest that it ever took place, nor to support recollections of old tramwaymen that railcoaches used to operate late-night dance specials into Blackpool from the Majestic Hotel at St Annes. Research has however brought to light one epic journey which might have been the foundation of the Ansdell "legend". The run was arranged, presumably by English Electric, for a party of Yorkshire transport managers led by Mr Harry England of West Riding; No 200 picked up the party at St Annes, where they were staying, and took them non-stop right through to Fleetwood. The journey from Fleetwood back to St Annes was completed in 45 minutes. This was the only recorded instance of a modern Blackpool car venturing on to the Lytham St Annes Corporation's rapidly disintegrating tracks south of Squires Gate. The Corporation did possess running rights to Lytham, but rarely exercised them in view of the state of the track. It was hoped eventually that through journeys from Lytham to Fleetwood would be possible under a unified Fylde tramway system, but in fact the nearest approach to this was a special Isle of Man Boat Tram from Lytham, introduced in August 1934. Although this was billed as a 17-mile tram service, passengers were only carried on the blue car as far as North Pier, where they had to buy a ticket at the Tramway Office in the pier entrance to cover the rest of the journey to Douglas. A Blackpool car would be waiting to take them to Fleetwood Ferry.

The autumn Illuminations of 1933 saw the old Fleetwood saloons in full cry for the last time. It was normal practice on Bank Holidays and Illuminations Saturdays to have every single vehicle out on the road, and this is meant quite literally; not one tram or bus would remain in the depôts or the works, and vehicles could be seen running half-painted and without windows if necessary. Saturday October 1 1933 was the last occasion when all 45 surviving Fleetwood cars were operated, eight from Blundell Street and the rest from Bispham.

The summer service finished on October 23 and with it ended the most intense period of activity in Bispham depôt's history. In the new winter timetable the Promenade service was to be run from Blundell Street as it had been before 1928, though photographic evidence suggests that Fleetwood Box cars were transferred to Blundell Street to work most of the Promenade duties. The winter schedules on the town routes already called for a maximum of 35 double-deckers and, since there were only 38 vestibuled Standard cars in stock at Marton and Blundell Street, it seems unlikely that there would be any spare double-deckers to operate the eight Promenade duties, without using the older open-fronted cars.

Transfer of the Promenade service to Blundell Street reduced pressure on Bispham's rolling stock sufficiently for four of the old saloons to be broken up in November 1933—eight-window Box 105, six-window Box 107 and Glasshouses 116 and 119. The upholstered seats from 105 and 107 were put aside to help re-equip Box cars 112-115. Company cars were still used on the Tramroad, notably on the Cleveleys turnbacks and Saturday specials, though the basic eight-car Fleetwood service was comfortably handled by the Pantograph cars. There was still no sign of the new railcoach making its debut on the Fleetwood route, for which ostensibly it was intended; instead, from November 18 it was placed on the Gynn—Squires Gate service.

Part 14: The veterans retire

ON the evening of December 23 1933, the first two new production railcoaches from English Electric, 201 and 202, entered service on the Promenade route. On January 6, No 203 appeared and thereafter the new cars arrived at approximately two-day intervals. The final chapter in the service life of the Fleetwood Tramroad cars had begun.

The Ministry of Transport inspection of the new railcoaches took place on January 9, when Col Anderson rode from Blundell Street to Clifton Drive, up to Bispham and back to the depôt. Rather surprisingly, he did not take the new car on to the stretch of tramroad north of Bispham which was laid without check rail. The length from Bispham to Cleveleys was in fact fitted with check rail shortly afterwards to permit double-deck running; this was one of the first permanent way jobs performed by the Tramways Department after they took over responsibility for the Promenade and Fleetwood reservations from the Highways Department in 1934. Curiously enough, a similar Ministry inspection in 1972 on a rebuilt one-man railcoach led to an enquiry by Col McNaughton as to the function of this angle-iron check rail and subsequent permission for its removal; the Transport Department had always regarded it as next to useless. Col Anderson was greatly impressed with the railcoach, remarking that the new cars were the finest thing he had seen in the transport world; they were like luxury coaches rather than trams.

One week after the inspection, the railcoaches made their debut on Dickson Road. On Monday, January 14 1934, two of the new cars, which were shedded at Blundell Street, were put on to North Station—Bispham turnbacks. Apart from one day in April 1926, it was the first time Blundell Street cars had worked on service along Dickson Road, though Standard double-deckers, probably from Marton, had operated special short-working duties at Easter 1933. The following day, the four-car Cleveleys service was turned over entirely to the railcoaches, including No 208 and 209 which were new in service that day.

This left Bispham depôt with only eight regular duties on the Fleetwood service, and three of the displaced Box cars, No 106, 108 and 109 were then broken up, leaving only ten Company saloons still in stock—eight-window Box cars 102 and 104, six-window cars 110 and 111, new Box cars 112-115 and the last surviving Glasshouses, 120 and 121. Some of these were holding the fort on the Promenade until the rest of the railcoaches arrived, whilst the remainder were in reserve for Tramroad specials.

By February 8 1934, fifteen of the new cars had arrived from Preston, and Walter Luff was able to put into effect the most dramatic improvement ever made to the Fleetwood service. The 10-minute service worked by eight Bispham Pantographs was summarily doubled. Fourteen cars were needed to operate a five-minute service; seven were Pantographs and seven were railcoaches from Blundell Street. Running time was cut to around 32 minutes, the nearest Mr Luff ever came to achieving the promised 30-minute journey. This acceleration proved to be a little over-ambitious; an extra railcoach was added to the service on February 18, and before long the journey time was back to the old 35-minute minimum. The Pantograph cars must have been struggling to keep up with this railcoach timetable. The railcoaches had 114 hp, compared to the Pantographs' 100 hp, and, according to the local press, one of the new cars had attained 60 miles/h during an official speed trial at night on a selected length of the Tramroad.

By the time the last of the railcoaches were being delivered in early March 1934, Box car 111 and Glasshouses 120 and 121 had disappeared, leaving only cars 102, 104, 110 and 112-115 still running. In little more than two months the railcoaches had achieved a virtual monopoly of the Promenade. When they took over the Squires Gate service on March 1, the new cars were operating five duties on the Lytham Road, six on the Promenade and eight on Fleetwood, which were worked by 23 single-deckers and one open-topped streamliner, No 226, running as a single-decker.

The last three old Box cars, 102, 104 and 110, were withdrawn after Easter when the Promenade service resumed double-deck operation, releasing the Promenade railcoaches for extra duties on the Fleetwood route. According to a somewhat unreliable Corporation document, Box car 110 was then classified as a "Fleetwood Tower Wagon", but the rest were quickly broken up to provide room for the expanding streamlined fleet. Demand for tram bodies as living quarters was not as high as it had been, and the Fleetwood cars were therefore dismantled, some of the timber being made into timetable frames. One car to escape was Glasshouse 120, which was taken down to the Transport Department football ground near the Lytham St Annes tram depôt in Squires Gate Lane, where it served until the war as a changing room, a position previously filled by the body of conduit car No 7.

According to the 'Gazette and Herald', some of the electrical equipment from cars scrapped that winter was used in the new open Boat cars 225-236, and it could be that some of the B18 controllers in those cars were taken from the Fleetwood Boxes. Upholstered seats from Box cars were used to re-equip Standard cars which were being converted from longitudinal seating; Crich cars 40 and 49 each have Fleetwood Box car seats in their lower saloon, from cars 108 and 106 respectively. Four sets of these seats were used to replace the wooden seats in the 1914 Box cars 112-115, which were the only Company saloons to survive the 1934 purge, probably because they were better able to maintain railcoach running speeds, being air-braked and having fairly new motors. Cars 112 and 113 had BTH 265 40-hp motors, 114 had the high-speed BTH 509 70-hp set, and 115 had the only pair of GE 67's in the Blackpool fleet.

The summer schedule of 1934 was the last to retain any semblance of the traditional Tramroad timetable. Bispham depôt provided a basic turnout of eleven cars, seven sharing the North Station—Fleetwood service with railcoaches from Blundell Street, and four on Cleveleys turnbacks. These Cleveleys trips were the last regular source of employment for the remaining Box cars 112-115.

Bispham had contrived to retain an air of independence from the other depôts, which made Blackpool crews refer to Bispham men as "the other firm". To many of the older staff, the shed remained much as it had been in Company days, tucked away down Red Bank Road, with the old generating station and Mr Cameron's house next door. But the writing was on the wall. The great Five Year Plan had no place for exclusive little tram depôts, at least not as year-round regular running sheds. To quote Walter Luff *"At Rigby Road there is a plot of land capable of housing the whole of the vehicles and men required for the Transport Department during at least eight months of the year . . . This would enable the whole of the summer vehicles to be stored at Marton and Bispham, and during the winter we should only have at Blundell Street and Rigby Road the vehicles actually required for the service, and not be hampered with other rolling stock".*

Work began in 1934 on a new £35 000 tram depôt, which was to be completed in time for the 1935 summer season. The new depôt was to be known as Kirby Hall, to denote the fact that it could also serve as an exhibition hall, using the side door in Kirby Road, and the depôt substation is still known today as Kirby Road substation.

The end of the old order came on October 22 1934. At 19.30 that evening, the last of the Box cars on the Cleveleys service ran down Red Bank Road to Bispham depôt. The depôt office then closed down, and the shed doors were shut for the winter. Inside were all 22 surviving Company cars, 112-115, 123-138, 140 and 141. Later that night the Pantographs, as they came off the Fleetwood service, were driven down to Blundell Street ready for the start of the winter timetable on the following day. For the first time ever, residents of Red Bank Road had to rouse themselves in the morning without the familiar sound of the Tramroad cars making their way up the single track to Bispham Top. Bispham was to remain closed as a

---

OPPOSITE
Above: On March 1 1934, the new production railcoaches took over the Lytham Road service from Gynn Square to Squires Gate. This Easter 1934 photograph shows car 223 standing at the Gynn.
(Dr H. A. Whitcombe, courtesy Science Museum

Below: Extension of check-rail to Cleveleys early in 1935 allowed open-top streamliners 237-249 to take over the Clifton Drive—Cleveleys service from June 8 1935. One is seen here at Clifton Drive terminus. (Dr H. A. Whitcombe, courtesy Science Museum

From 1934 the transverse upholstered seats from scrapped Fleetwood box cars were used to replace the longitudinal seats on one side of the lower saloon in many Standard cars. Standard car 40, now at Crich, has transverse seats from Fleetwood box car 108. (W. G. S. Hyde)

running shed until May 11 1940.

The winter schedules of 1934-5 included an extended Promenade service running between Clifton Drive and Cleveleys. It was not the first time this had been tried, for the Fleetwood Box cars had operated a short-lived Pleasure Beach—Cleveleys winter service in 1930, but it heralded a further incursion of the Tramroad by town cars. By this time, of course, it was difficult to distinguish a Tramroad car from any other.

For the older Fleetwood employees, each new time-table seemed to bring a further degradation of the Tramroad traditions, and the 1935 summer schedules, which came into effect on June 8, were no exception. On that day the Clifton Drive—Cleveleys service was taken over by the open-top streamliners 237-249, bringing double-deckers out of Blackpool territory for the first time. Bispham depôt remained closed until June 19, when four cars, probably the Box cars, were dusted down and brought out for the day. Any notions that the old saloons would be called upon regularly were soon quashed, however, by the entry into service two days later of the first of 20 new railcoaches, No 264 to 283.

When these new railcoaches were ordered, in December 1934, Walter Luff had announced that they were to replace the Fleetwood racks. Fortunately this did not happen. The opening of "Kirby Hall" provided ample depôt space for the new cars, and the intended purchase of the Lytham St Annes system included an undertaking to relay the track between Squires Gate and St Annes and equip it with modern cars. The Fleetwood racks survived and helped to cater for unprecedented traffic levels on the Fleetwood route during the 1935 season. On July 30, no less than 60 cars were running on the Fleetwood route, and the first night of the Illuminations, September 14, set a record which was never equalled. On that night the number of trams operated by the Corporation reached the staggering total of 224, including the Gondola and Lifeboat and 25 hired from Lytham St Annes.

With the opening of the new depôt, Blundell Street shed was given over largely to the Fleetwood route, and the old Bispham staff soon managed to re-establish their air of independence. Tramroad traditions suffered another blow, however, at the end of the 1935 summer service, when the majority of the Pantograph cars were put into store. There were now sufficient railcoaches in stock to maintain all the winter services, apart from Marton and Layton. The annual mileage of the Pantographs fell from over 50 000 to 25 000, and was not to return to a respectable level until the end of the war.

The Pantographs were back in business for the summer of 1936, and during the season Dickson Road passengers grew accustomed to the sight of Standard cars from Marton depôt running up Talbot Road to run extra duties as far as Bispham. But the four surviving Fleetwood Box cars were rarely to be seen. Their final appearance, still in the old red livery, was on North Station — Cleveleys specials on Illuminations Saturdays. To a travelling public used by then to the streamlined luxury of the railcoach fleet, they must have seemed like half-forgotten relics of a vanished era on the Tramroad. Which indeed they were. The four Box cars were used for the last time on October 10 1936, and in the following year cars 113 and 115 were broken up, leaving 112 and 114 as Permanent Way Gang cars.

These were the first Fleetwood scrappings for three years, and as yet there was no sign of any move to replace the Fleetwood racks, which now seemed likely, against all earlier expectations, to survive the Five Year Plan almost unscathed. Even the arrival of 20 more railcoaches, 284 to 303, had little effect. Cars 135 and 137 were relegated to works car duties during 1937, and 141 became the new illuminated Progress car, but traffic on the Fleetwood route was growing so quickly that a new substation had to be built at Copse Road to increase the capacity of the line. A few days after this was opened, a full muster of 15 Fleetwood racks was operated from Bispham on July 30 1937; these would be cars 123-134, 136, 138 and 140. Seven days later, the barely credible total of 83 cars ran on the Fleetwood route.

The summer of 1938 followed a very similar course to that of 1937 and, although the Czechoslovak crisis put rather a damper on the latter part of the holiday season, traffic was still sufficient to require the Fleetwood racks from time to time. At the end of the season 130 and 138 were broken up, and the demise of the rest was confirmed in January 1939 when a tender was accepted for twelve English Electric single-deckers which would be a modernised version of the old open cars. The 13 Fleetwood survivors, No 123-129, 131-134, 136 and 140 would run for just one more summer.

Their final summer season in 1939 was rather an anti-climax. No trams ran from Bispham depôt until August, when 16 Blackpool open toastracks emerged from store. By this time the season was drawing to a premature end, as the declaration of war became inevitable, and the entry into service of car No 10, the first of the new open-sided cars, seemed some-

The last Fleetwood cross-bench cars were replaced in 1939 by twelve new semi-open railcoaches built by English Electric, No 10-21, of which No 12 (shown above) featured in English Electric publicity. These cars had secondhand electrical equipment, wooden seats, waist-high sliding doors, minimum lighting, no partition between driver and passengers, and had the upper half of the windows unglazed. They were rebuilt in 1942 with full windows, doors and cabs.
(English Electric catalogue

thing of an irrelevance. As far as is known, the 13 Fleetwood racks never ran at all in 1939; their last day in service was October 22 1938, though nobody realised it at the time. More than 20 years were to pass before passengers would once again ride on a car of the Blackpool & Fleetwood Tramroad Company.

Part 15: The Pantographs' Indian Summer

WHEN we last mentioned the Pantograph cars 167-176, they had been relegated to summer use only with the arrival of the second-series railcoaches in 1935. It looked as though the Pantographs, only seven years old, were on the way out, though in cost-conscious Blackpool they would not have been withdrawn entirely before the £20 000 loan for their purchase was repaid in 1943. Car 167 was already listed as Engineering Car for the winter of 1935-36, a rôle which it was later to assume permanently. To complete the story of the Fleetwood Tramroad cars in Blackpool, we will now see how these most distinctive of tramcars managed to remain in passenger service for another quarter of a century.

The story of the Pantograph cars in the mid-1930's is curiously similar to that of the Blackpool toastracks related in *Modern Tramway* for September 1973. Both classes had managed to survive the initial phase of scrappings in 1933-35 and had been repainted in the new livery, with a green-and-cream version of the old red-and-white colour scheme. Like the Standard cars, they represented a sort of mid-point between the condemned cars, which were left in red and white until they were scrapped, and the new streamlined fleet, which carried a predominantly cream colour scheme. None of these cars conformed to the new tenets of centre-entrance with low platforms which the Transport Department had decided were the modern answer to the problems of slow loading and unloading, but none were scheduled for early withdrawal since they provided that extra capacity which was essential in summer, but which would not have warranted the purchase of brand-new cars.

In 1936, with the end of the Five Year Plan in sight and the political climate beginning to swing towards the retention of trams on all routes except Layton and Central Drive, the Transport Department began a programme to refurbish the toastracks and Pantographs and give them at least a vague resemblance to the new fleet. Rigby Road works was underemployed at the time, since the new streamlined cars were not due for first overhauls, and there was plenty of capacity available to complete both classes of car during 1936 and 1937. The toastrack cars were dealt with first, but in the Spring of 1936 three Pantographs, 167, 169 and 175, were repainted experimentally in a new livery which appears from a distant postcard view to have been largely cream, with a green roof and cream trolley mast, almost the reverse of the 1933 green Pantograph livery which had a green clerestory and trolley mast

Blackpool Pantograph car 171 in its post-1937 cream livery, photographed at Gynn Square in July, 1945
(D. Conrad, courtesy TMS

on a cream roof. Both these colour schemes proved to be short-lived.

At the end of the 1936 season, car 167 returned to the works for a more comprehensive refurbishing which was completed in January, and the rest of the class followed until car 169 was finished in October 1937. The main object seemed to be to disguise them as railcoaches—a fairly hopeless exercise in camouflage—and the new livery was almost entirely cream, with the green confined to the roof, the window frames and the clerestory window frames. Perhaps the most comical aspect of the camouflage was the removal of the large front numerals and their replacement by small shaded transfer numerals placed halfway down the car, just above where the centre entrance would have been, if there had been a centre entrance.

The changes to the Pantographs were mainly structural. The rather amateurish destination box was replaced by an unusually curvaceous design which harmonised nicely with the contours of the roof, and the old wooden windscreens gave way to a very neat Auster metal-framed screen with Trico air-operated wipers. Folding doors were added to the platforms, and this allowed the platform seats to be upholstered. Inside the car all the brass handles were chromium plated to reduce the incidence of skin disease amongst the guards, whilst the pantograph tower was reduced in height by 15 inches, presumably to achieve standardisation in the stock of trolley heads and by eliminating different angles between trolley pole and overhead wire. The only mechanical improvement was the replacement of the original G. D. Peters air-brake controls by the Westinghouse type with quick-release valve and silencer, to give quicker getaway from stops. All the modernised cars were turned out in the new "railcoach" livery, which they were to keep until the end of the war, long after the railcoaches themselves had lost it.

The Pantographs stayed on summer-only workings from Blundell Street/Rigby Road until 1940. They are rather better documented than the original Fleetwood vehicles, but their pre-war career still contains a touch of mystery which it may be well to expound at this point, in case some reader may be able to enlighten us. In an earlier section the author expressed his conviction that the Pantograph cars never operated away from the Dickson Road route other than for depôt journeys; this was based on the absence of documentary or photographic evidence, and the fact that the destination blinds were limited to the North Station—Fleetwood route. It came as something of a surprise, therefore, to discover recently a photograph taken in 1935, showing a Pantograph car, large as life, about to pass a blue Lytham St. Annes car on the Promenade between Manchester Square and the Pleasure Beach. Was it a works car, a special duty, or did Pantographs regularly operate on the Promenade? Not for the first (or last) time in this history, the author must admit his ignorance and appeal to the reader for information.

One duty reserved for the Pantographs was the Fleetwood local service, which had been introduced on July 25 1941 after complaints from Fleetwood that residents were being crowded off the trams in summer by through passengers. The local service comprised two Pantographs shuttling between Fleetwood Ferry and Broadwater, a point which had not previously featured on the Tramroad destination blinds. To avoid burdening the crews on this none-too-popular duty with having to change four destination blinds every ten minutes, the dual destination "Broadwater and Fleetwood" was added to the front and rear blinds, rather in the manner that the cars in Company days had "Blackpool and Fleetwood" painted on each end. Cars on the North Station route carried the number 1 on the side blinds and, to distinguish the Fleetwood locals, their side blinds were turned to read "Fleetwood Only".

On the question of the "Fleetwood Only" destination, new research has thrown more light on the origins of this display, which was mentioned in Part 10 of this history. It seems that in June 1927 Fleetwood Council complained that passengers for Rossall and Fleetwood were being crowded off the through cars by short-distance passengers. According to the 'Gazette & Herald':

"The provision of special cars labelled 'Fleetwood Only', and others for intermediate stations, should remedy matters and it is understood that the necessary arrangements will be made."

These cars apparently became known as "Fleetwood Officials", and were still running in 1935, as evidenced by the experience of an 'Evening Gazette' reader:

"I had to travel from Lowther Avenue to Bispham, a distance of 500 yards. Several cars passed full and eventually I boarded one bound for Fleetwood. I offered my legal penny, or twopence if the car has run on the Promenade pre-

vious to reaching the Gynn. The conductor demanded sixpence. He said it was the minimum fare, as the car was a 'Fleetwood Official'."

The curious anomaly of charging a minimum of twopence on Promenade cars north of the Gynn, against the normal penny on Dickson Road cars, is the likeliest explanation of the practice which developed of showing "1" on the front blinds of railcoaches and the side blinds of Pantographs when they were running on the North Station line. Knowing residents at least could then avoid paying 2d for a 1d ride on the Tramroad; perhaps the "1" originally indicated "1d fare"? In later years the "1" was used permanently on the Pantographs, and my colleague, Mr G. S. Palmer, recalls an occasion when he was guard on a Pantograph car and in a nostalgic moment turned the side blind to "Norbreck Cleveleys & Fleetwood", only to be ordered peremptorily by the inspector at Bispham Station to *"turn that b---- blind back to '1'."*

The cream livery had begun to disappear from the railcoaches in 1941, giving way to a mainly green colour scheme with a splendid cream "V" at the front to render the otherwise rather dark vehicle more conspicuous in the blackout. A few Pantographs were repainted in 1944-45, but it seems that these were still turned out in the 1936 cream livery, and it was not until late in 1945 that the first Pantographs appeared in the contemporary railcoach livery. Stylistically the application of this streamlined colour scheme to the Pantographs' more traditional bodywork ought to have looked bizarre, as it did when applied experimentally to Standard cars, but somehow the cream "V" blended admirably with the rounded lines of the body, and today few enthusiasts can envisage the Pantographs wearing any other livery.

On May 11 1940, Bispham depôt reopened as a running shed after the requisitioning of Marton depôt, and the Pantographs returned to their original home. At first they saw little if any winter duty but, as the war went on, with maintenance problems and the high level of vehicle usage all the year round, the theoretical excess of trams was gradually reduced and the Pantographs crept back more and more into the winter scene. By 1945 they were clocking up annual mileages of over 40 000, almost double the miles they had been running before the war.

The twelve semi-open cars, No 10-21,

which had been bought in 1939 to replace the Fleetwood racks, had not proved to be a very good investment. They served little purpose at a time when visitors were few and far between, and in 1942 they had been rebuilt as totally-enclosed "sun saloons". Their main use during the rest of the war was as troop carriers, but in peacetime their wooden seats hardly endeared them to the returning holidaymakers and although they were a fairly frequent sight on the Fleetwood route, they spent much of their time in Bispham depôt.

In January 1948, car 10 was rebuilt with upholstered seats and fluorescent lights and transferred to Marton depôt, where it was followed eventually by sister cars 11-15, the last-named being completed in October 1949. The next car to be transferred, No 21, was fitted with new Maley & Taunton resilient-wheel bogies, and this of course released its original English Electric bogies for possible further use. When these were removed in March 1949 they had accumulated only 29 200 miles since they were new in 1939. These bogies were used to replace those under car 10; No 9's bogies went under No 15; 15's under 16, and eventually the spare pair emerged from under 16 and was placed under Standard car 39.

The experiment with 39 proved unsuccessful and, since the Marton "Vambac" rebuildings were intended to release a further 11 pairs of virtually new bogies from the remaining sun saloons, it was decided to experiment with Pantograph car 173. The car entered service on July 4 1950 and was adjudged to be successful enough for the remaining Pantographs to be similarly equipped as the English Electric bogies were released. Car 172 was the last to be completed, but 167 and 176 were never done.

The cars were lifted in Blundell Street depôts whilst the bogies were changed, and the fourth to arrive was No 176 on October 3 1950, which was intended to receive the bogies from sun saloon No 17. It never did; in fact it never returned from Blundell Street. No official version ever emerged of the events surrounding 176's demise, but what seems to have happened is this. Walter Luff had been discussing the possible application of the passenger-flow system at Blackpool, and apparently Frank Hirst, the Chief Engineer, decided to experiment with one of the Pantograph cars. Accordingly 176 was taken into the body shop, one of its doors was panelled over, and a new door built on the opposite side of the platform. It is said that Mr Luff, on seeing the partly-finished car during his rounds of the workshops, immediately put a stop to the job. No provision had been made at that stage for a seated conductor, and the panelling remained unpainted. Unfortunately no clear photographs have come to light of 176 in its rebuilt state, and details of the work carried out remain uncertain. Can any reader help?

The lack of photographs is surprising, since 176 did not disappear quickly. On November 10 1950, 176 was moved back into Blundell Street, where it was decided to use the car as depôt shunter, organising the rows of redundant and derelict Standard cars which had been building up in the shed since the war and which were now to be scrapped. Odd parts of 176 were cannibalised, including its compressor which went into 168, and eventually

In 1950-51 eight of the ten Blackpool Pantograph cars were remounted on English Electric bogies taken from Vambac cars 10-21. Retrucked car 172 is seen above at Fleetwood Ferry; the lower picture shows the standard English Electric bogie built for Blackpool in 1933-39.
(C. Carter, TMS Collection

its No 1 motor which was "borrowed" for 174 in July 1953. 176 continued its occasional duties as shunter until one day it suffered a fault in its solitary motor just as it was passing through the narrow depôt entrance. Apparently at that moment an emergency call was received for one of the ambulances which were then housed in the shed. The upshot of this was that 176 was banished in disgrace to the scrap line, and on September 18 1954 was broken up.

No 176 was one of three Pantograph cars put on the scrapping list on July 23 1954, though it was the only one of the three actually to be dismantled. Car 169, which had taken the bogies from car 10 in May 1951, was out of service and gradually degenerating into a derelict condition. Some Transport Department records show 169 as being scrapped in 1954, but in fact this car was overhauled and returned to service in September of that year.

In rather worse straits was car 167, which was the only one of the class still retaining its Preston bogies, having been given a truck overhaul in November 1949, the last to be done before the change of bogies began. 167 had been idle since 1953, having accumulated the impressive mileage of 133 200 miles since overhaul, and had lost a motor to car 175 in July of that year. Like 169, car 167 was officially scrapped but was actually converted in September 1954 into a permanent way car to take over from ex-Company crossbench car 6 and largely to supersede the Box car, PW 5. "Converted" is perhaps not the right term since 167 was little changed from its service days, retaining its passenger livery and number, the only visible alteration being the legend "Permanent Way" on the destination boxes. Since one of its motors had already been "borrowed" and the car was not to return to passenger service, a pair of the less powerful 35-hp BTH B265C motors, of the type fitted to the Standard cars, was mounted on the car's original Preston bogies. This made an odd contrast to the other cars, which had new bogies but with the old motors.

The arrival of the 25 Coronation cars in 1952/53 meant the end of all-year running for the Pantographs, and the end of the most intensive period of running in their entire careers. To illustrate this remarkable "second wind", car 171 had run a total of 176 490 miles between September 1935 and July 1942, an average of 26 000 miles per year. From then until receiving its new bogies in October 1950, 171 clocked up 351 700 miles at a yearly average of 41 000 miles.

Blackpool 167 at Copse Road depôt in postwar green and cream livery, retaining its original trucks and used as a Permanent Way gang car. On the right in this 1955 photograph is the electric locomotive. (R. Brook, block courtesy Tramway Museum Society.

The new turning loop at Little Bispham in 1937, on a newly-reconstructed portion of the Fleetwood tramroad. The road at the right was also new, having been opened in March 1932 as the final link in the direct coast road from Blackpool to Fleetwood.
(Blackpool Transport Dept)

Part 16: Active retirement

WHEN the Second World War began, 13 of the old Company crossbench cars were still waiting in Bispham depôt in case, by some miracle, the holiday season recovered sufficiently for them to be needed on the Tramroad. They might well have stayed there for years, had the Government not requisitioned Marton depôt for the production of aircraft components. Before Marton closed on November 3, room had to be found for the cars which were normally housed there. Besides the Marton trams, eight new cars, No 14 to 21, were due to be delivered from English Electric, who had refused the Corporation's request to store them at Preston until the 1940 season.

There was no alternative but to scrap some of the older vehicles, and so, during the autumn of 1939, seven of the Fleetwood cars were broken up in the yard at Copse Road. These were Box car 112, crossbench cars 131 and 140, ex-trailer 136 and all three of the majestic Vanguards, 123-125. The scrapping of the Vanguards is difficult to explain, since they were the most modern of all the Fleetwood vehicles and the only open cars with drivers' windscreens and Preston bogies. The surviving Corporation records, unreliable at the best of times, are contradictory on the scrapping dates of three other Fleetwood cars, No 129, 134 and 135, and it is possible that

Blackpool and Fleetwood box car 40 before and after its 1960 restoration. Numbered 114 from 1920 to 1942, this car then became Permanent Way car No 5, based at Rigby Rd. (A. K. Terry and R. F. Mack)

This history originally appeared in serial form in Modern Tramway, 1974-6, and was intended to cover the development of the Fleetwood Tramroad and its cars from 1920 up to the point where the Tramroad lost its separate identity and became part of the integrated Blackpool system. Chapters 1 to 4 cover briefly the early history of the line up to the Corporation take-over. Chapter 1 incorporates portions of D. F. Phillips' history of the Tramroad, 1898-1920, which appeared in Tramway Review No. 25 (LRTL, 1958). Chapter 2 is taken from a new study of this period currently being prepared by Brian Turner.

they too were broken up at the same time. Both 129 and 135 are noted as having been works cars around this period, but precise dates are not recorded.

There is no doubt, however, that most of the surviving Fleetwood single-deckers did become works cars. "Old Opens" 126, 132 and 133 and ex-trailer 137 were assigned to the Permanent Way department, whilst Box car 114 was the PW gang car. Two more 1898 crossbench cars, 127 and 128, were kept as snowploughs, carrying the large "V" ploughs which had been inherited from the Tramroad Company; these would naturally have been designed to fit the Company's open cars, which performed as works cars during the winter months.

By a neat stroke of fate, 127 and 128 had been assigned to their new rôle for only a few months when the tramway system suffered the worst snowfall in its entire history. The snow began falling on the evening of January 27 1940, and by 22.00 the drifts were so deep that ten trams had to be abandoned where they stood—seven Standards between Talbot Square and Devonshire Square, one railcoach in Dickson Road and two more in Lord Street, Fleetwood.

It was January 30 before the first trams — four Standard cars — appeared, running between Talbot Square and Manchester Square. At 15.30 on February 1, a single line was opened as far as Rossall, and the Fleetwood route was cleared by the following day. The last section to be reopened was the Promenade south of Manchester Square; Mr J. R. Henson, one of the early Blackpool enthusiasts and author of the first published history of the system, was living at South Shore at the time:

"*We kept hearing rumours, day by day — 'the snowploughs are at Alexandra Road', 'the snowploughs are at Station Road'. When they did arrive at the South Promenade they consisted of two Fleetwood racks, 127 and 128. Coupled behind 127 was Pantograph car 176 whilst 128 was linked to Fleetwood box car 114, one pair of cars on each track. Their method of operation was to run back about 50 yards from the snowdrift and then accelerate. As they hit the snow their momentum carried them about 20 yards before they were brought to a standstill. Then they reversed and started again.*"

South Promenade was finally cleared on February 4, seven days after the snow had fallen.

Around 1942—the exact date is not known—the surviving Fleetwood cars were "rationalised". Old Opens 126 and 132 and Box car 114 were repainted in all-over green and numbered in the Permanent Way fleet, No 3, 6 and 5 respectively. The two snowploughs, 127 and 128, retained their green-and-cream passenger livery and their old numbers, whilst 133 and 137, the last ex-trailer, were broken up.

So it was that the Fleetwood Tramroad, as it completed its first half-century in 1948, still witnessed the occasional comings and goings of four of its first ten cars—crossbench No 1, 2, 3 and 7— and one of its last, Box car 40. This must have been very gratifying for the older staff who had worked for the Tramroad Company, though it is debatable whether the Permanent Way staff were equally enthusiastic about some of the vehicles they had to drive each winter.

This pleasant state of affairs continued until October 1951, when PW car No 3 (Corporation car 126 and Tramroad car 1) was broken up in Blundell Street car shed. Snowplough 128 was also stored in Blundell Street, where it was scrapped in October 1952, whilst No 127, the other snowplough, was at Copse Road. Also at Fleetwood was No 6 (ex-132, ex-7) which usually served as a gang car, being partic-

Blackpool and Fleetwood 2 as restored in 1960, after serving for 21 years as snowplough car 127.
(R. F. Mack)

ularly useful for storing the track men's bicycles. No 6 was dismantled in February 1955, leaving only two Company cars in stock—PW gang car No 5 (ex-114, ex-40) which operated from Rigby Road, and crossbench car 127, in store at Fleetwood.

In 1959 the ranks of the ex-Company cars were increased to approximately $2\frac{1}{2}$, when the superstructure of the illuminated "Progress" car was removed to reveal crossbench car 141, incongruously sporting a railcoach trolley tower on its venerable clerestory roof. After languishing for some months at the back of Rigby Road, 141 was taken up to Copse Road in May 1960. In February 1961, No 141 returned to the workshops to be rebuilt into the illuminated "Rocket". The doubtful wisdom of this, in view of the number of other cars which were becoming redundant, soon became apparent and the beginnings of "Tramnik One" were removed from 141's frame and mounted on Pantograph car 168. 141's ancient plate-frame bogies were sent to Crich, and the other remains were scrapped.

Meanwhile a happier fate had befallen the other Fleetwood survivors. On February 5 1960, crossbench car 127 was brought out of Copse Road and driven down to the works to be restored for the celebration of the 75th Anniversary of the Blackpool tramways. Since the car was intended to run in service, the restoration had to be a compromise between authenticity and legality, which meant that the electric headlights had to be retained. This, combined with the use of Corporation style numerals and some rather freelance lining on the dash panels, gave the ends of the car a slightly unconvincing appearance when repainted in Tramroad Company colours, but otherwise it was a very creditable restoration on a limited budget.

The original celebration plans had allowed for the restoration of three cars —the other two were the 1885 conduit car No 4 (alias No 1) and the Dreadnought No 59—but at the last minute it was decided to extend the scheme to include Permanent Way car 5, which duly emerged with its original number as Tramroad box car No 40. As with the crossbench car, the body details remained pure 1930-style, which made the Tramroad livery somewhat anachronistic to the purist. Not that such niceties were of any importance at the time, though it would be gratifying to see an accurate restoration of the Box car to 1931 livery to match its upholstered interior and high-speed motors.

The two restored cars returned to passenger service on July 29 1960. The crossbench car, No 2, was mainly used on Promenade Circulars, but Box 40 was more often running Fleetwood specials, particularly on market days. Crews, passengers and enthusiasts alike were somewhat taken aback by the Box car's turn of speed—it still retained its experimental 70-hp motors from 1928. These weeks in the late summer of 1960 represented a high point of the Fleetwood Tramroad, for the route was being operated by all four types of car which had provided the basic service since the opening of the line—Box car, Pantograph, Railcoach and Coronation.

Perhaps the most remarkable fact of all was that the Pantographs were still there, a quarter century after Walter Luff had relegated them to second-class status. Ever since the Coronation cars arrived in the early 1950's, it had seemed as if the Pantographs must disappear soon, but each summer they emerged again from Bispham depôt. To the local enthusiasts there was a particular thrill about the first appearance of the old green cars each Good Friday, after the relative monotony of the winter service. The Pantographs personified the unique sense of continuity attached to the North Station—Fleetwood route, as they swept impressively along Dickson Road, trolley ropes billowing out behind, just as Fleetwood cars had done for sixty years or more.

The Pantographs remained smart right to the end; the entire class was in fact repainted as late as 1957, including the PW car No 167, which re-appeared in the standard works car livery of all-green. The eight passenger cars, 168-175, retained their splendid green livery with large cream "V"; this was surprising, since Mr J. C. Franklin, who had taken over as manager from Walter Luff in 1954, had already removed the "V" from most of the other passenger cars.

Internally the Pantographs were less than immaculate. In 1960 one passenger wrote to the 'Evening Gazette':

"*This is a plea from those Grand Old Ladies of the track who are brought out each season from their well-earned retirement to help their younger sisters on route No 1. It seems that they feel keenly the lack of renovations and repairs, and the remarks of passengers not willing to sit, lest they should soil their new holiday clothing, and the language also of some who suddenly contact the business end of a spring which almost comes through the worn-out upholstery. They point out, too,*

Fleetwood racks

Above: Workmen strip the brass handrails from condemned cars 124, 136 and 137 outside Copse Road depôt in September 1939.
(A. R. Spencer

Centre: Rack 132 became Permanent Way car 6 in 1942 and ran until 1955, taking the PW gang (and their bicycles) to and from Copse Road. It is seen here at Rigby Road in July 1945.
(D. Conrad

Below: Rack 128 was retained as a snowplough until 1952, and similar car 127 survived until 1960 at Copse Road and was then restored as Tramroad No 2. This 1950 photograph at Blundell Street also shows permanent way car 3, ex-126, which was scrapped in 1951. (J. Copland

that although they still possess most of the energy and activity of their younger sisters, they feel ashamed when would-be passengers more or less politely step back as they approach, to wait for the next car. Gallantly doing their stuff between North Station and Fleetwood, some action should be taken as soon as possible to relieve their evident distress."

The 75th Anniversary on September 29 1960 provided a fitting climax to the career of the Pantograph cars. A procession of eleven trams was arranged, to run from Pleasure Beach to Little Bispham and back. Besides the four restored cars, the other main classes of tram were included, the Pantographs being represented by No 170. One of the most interesting features of the anniversary procession was that 170 travelled from Bispham depôt to the Pleasure Beach and back as a Promenade special, carrying fare-paying passengers to South Shore for the first time since before the war.

From the high point of September 29 1960, the Pantographs went into a rapid decline. The decision to abandon the Lytham Road route at the end of the next season made it unlikely that the Pantographs would last more than another summer, and it was no great surprise to learn in January 1961 that four of the class had been withdrawn—No 169, 171, 173 and 174. 174 had spent the whole of 1960 in store at the back of Rigby Road depôt. The remaining four Pantographs were prepared for a further season, having their paintwork touched up and generally looking extremely smart.

During January 1961, the terminus at North Station was cut back from the station entrance, where the trams had reversed since 1920, to the site of the old Company terminus of 1898. The new layout included a trolley reverser, designed for fixed trolley heads and a great rarity thereby. Since trolley ropes were an embarrassment at reversers, the four Pantograph cars, No 168, 170, 172 and 175, lost their ropes and were fitted instead with a collapsible bamboo pole which was secreted away inside the body framework.

The appearance of car 170 for driver training duties on March 10 1961 seemed a good omen for the new summer season but, when Good Friday arrived, only two cars, 172 and 175, emerged from Bispham depôt. The Bispham crews obviously had little faith in the ability of the Pantographs to negotiate the new trolley reverser, since they meticulously swung the trolley by hand and placed it on the exit wire from the reverser. The appearance of only two cars at Easter did not augur well for the rest of the summer, but it still came as a surprise to learn in May that the licences of the four serviceable cars had been allowed to lapse, although 170 and 172 were officially "in reserve" at Bispham. 170 made the last passenger-carrying run by a Pantograph, for an enthusiasts' tour on October 15 1961.

Part 17: Preservation

THE announcement that the Pantograph cars would not be operated during the 1961 summer season was taken with more than a pinch of salt by local enthusiasts. After all, it was unusual in Blackpool—and anywhere else, come to that—for an entire class of vehicles to be withdrawn almost at a single stroke. So it was confidently expected that at least a few Pantographs would be brought out of retirement at the height of the season, in the same way as the surviving Standard cars had been used since losing their last regular duties in 1954. Four Pantographs—170, 171, 172 and 175 —were actually held in store at Bispham depôt for just such a contingency.

Any doubts about the other Pantographs were removed on May 19 when four English Electric railcoaches arrived from Rigby Road to take their place. As part of a general shuffle of the tram fleet ready for the start of the summer timetable on the following day, four open "Boats" moved round from Marton depôt to fill the space at Rigby Road, leaving room at Marton for three of the withdrawn Pantographs, 169, 173 and 174. It was the first time Pantographs had ever been housed there, and yet the green single-deckers looked entirely at home beside the double-deck Standards which shared the right-hand side of the shed. The fourth withdrawn car, No 168, was taken to Rigby Road works, where it replaced crossbench car 141 as the foundation for the illuminated Rocket "Tranmik One". Little remained of 168 after the operation—basically the underframe, bogies, motors and one air-brake column.

Hopes of a Pantograph revival in the high season turned out to be optimistic, and only No 170 out of the four "reserve" cars ever ran again, and that solely for enthusiasts' tours. It was, however, still possible to catch the occasional glimpse of a Pantograph in action, for the all-green Permanent Way car No 167 was transferred to Rigby Road depôt to replace the old gang car which had been restored as Box car 40 for the 75th anniversary. 167's return to the limelight after six years of obscurity at Copse Road, was crowned at the end of the 1961 season by it selection as the first Blackpool tram to be preserved in a British museum. The choice of 167 rather than one of the more serviceable cars at Bispham was justified on the ground that the PW car was the only member of the class to retain its original Preston bogies, though conversely its BTH265C motors were some way removed from the genuine 50-hp GEC equipment. 167 left for Crich Museum on May 17 1962, but has not yet run under its own power there.

167's place as Permanent Way car was taken by the last operational Pantograph, No 170, minus half its seats to replace those missing from 167. Apart from showing the destination "Permanent way" —a source of some puzzlement amongst intending passengers during the holiday season—170 looked all the world like the traditional Pantograph car, and the sight of its distinctive cream-V colour scheme on the Tramroad helped to dispel a little of the gloom which was beginning to settle over the Blackpool tramway system.

By April 1962, a year had passed since the Pantographs last ran in service and yet, apart from No 168, not one of the cars had been scrapped, 170 was based at Copse Road, 171, 172 and 175 were stored at Bispham, and 167, 169, 173 and 174 were stored at Marton. The first to go were 169 and 173, broken up in Marton depôt during April. No 174 managed to avoid the scrapmen, however, and to make up the quota Marton depôt's Vambac railcoach No 208 was sent to Bispham on April 30, and returned dragging behind it car 171 which was dismantled during the following week.

No 174 meanwhile had been chosen for the Department's most ambitious illuminated tram, the "Sante Fe" train. Using a spare set of Willison couplers left over when the twin-car conversion programme was cut from twelve cars to ten, the Pantograph was coupled to an "engine" rebuilt from railcoach No 209. 174 was perfectly fitted for the rôle of Santa Fe carriage, since its distinctive curved clresory roof was derived originally from the standard American railroad car. Very little alteration was made to the body structure of 174, the most obvious change being the rebuilding of the ends to simulate a typical American observation car, whilst inside the car the old seating was replaced by Belgian-style back-to-back double seats. Until recently it was the practice on the opening night of the Illuminations to remove some of the seats and install a bar inside the tram to entertain the official party on their tour of the lights.

When the Santa Fe train was completed in time for the 1962 Illuminations, there were still two Pantographs in Bispham depôt, but neither survived for long. No 172 had been earmarked as the next illuminated tram, but was replaced by railcoach 222 and broken up at Rigby Road in February 1963, whilst 175 met the same fate in the same month at Marton. The sole survivor, PW car 170, sadly lasted only two more years before being chosen as the basis for the illuminated "HMS Blackpool" in 1965. This time nothing recognisable remained of the Pantograph, and to all intents and purposes the class was extinct in Blackpool. It was a little ironic that the cars which remained intact—167 at Crich, and 174 as the Santa Fe coach—where the two Pantographs which had been out of passenger service on the final years of the class: 168 had been a works car, and 174 was unserviceable or, in Blackpool parlance, "demic".

The scrapping of the Pantographs was only part of a massive upheaval which, between 1961 and 1963, produced the greatest transformation in Blackpool's transport since Walter Luff swept through the Department in the 1930's. The retirement of several long-serving officers, mainly tramwaymen, was followed by a programme of "rationalisation" in which the street routes were abandoned, outlying depôts closed, rolling stock scrapped in large numbers, and efforts made to integrate bus and tram maintenance and operation.

In this new "rational' climate, the museum cars, so recently the pride of the Department, seemed to be regarded more as an encumbrance occupying valuable depôt space. The last two Tramroad Company cars, crossbench No 2 and Box car 40, spent their final years in Blackpool being shunted from depôt to depôt like aged ancestors being accommodated

Above: Blackpool and Fleetwood Box car 40 in passenger service at the Pleasure Beach on July 31 1960, during the 75th anniversary season of Blackpool's tramways. The car is now at the TMS store at Clay Cross, Derbyshire.
(R. Brook

Below: Blackpool and Fleetwood 2 is now the mainstay of the summer school party traffic at Crich since it can carry up to 80 young children and also act as a mobile classroom, with the guide/lecturer/conductor standing alongside.
(J. H. Price

by a succession of reluctant relatives. Their first move came in December 1960 when they were driven from Rigby Road to Marton for storage—probably the first time a Fleetwood Box car had been inside the shed, though several racks are said to have been stored there just before the war.

The restored cars remained at Marton all through the summer of 1961, frustrating hopes that the previous year's museum car service would become an annual event. Public operation in 1961 amounted to just two Promenade Circular trips by the Fleetwood rack after a television broadcast on July 8. At the end of the season the restored cars were dismissed to Copse Road shed, where it seemed they were likely to gather dust indefinitely. There was no sign of them the following season until August 2 when the Fleetwood rack suddenly reappeared at Central Station to take its place amongst the open Boat cars on the Promenade Circular. After several weeks' operation, No 2 went back into store but, since Copse Road was being cleared ready for closure, the rack spent most of the winter in the reopened shed at Blundell Street. Room was found for Box car 40 at Bispham, which meant that within two years the Fleetwood cars had been housed at all five depôts on the system.

Their wanderings were almost over, for in October 1962 the Corporation decided to offer the Fleetwood cars free of charge, along with several others, to the Tramway